Myths are public dreams, dreams are private myths.
Joseph Campbell

Human live through their myths and only endure their realities.
Robert Anton Wilson

CONTENTS

MINORU YANAGIHASHI

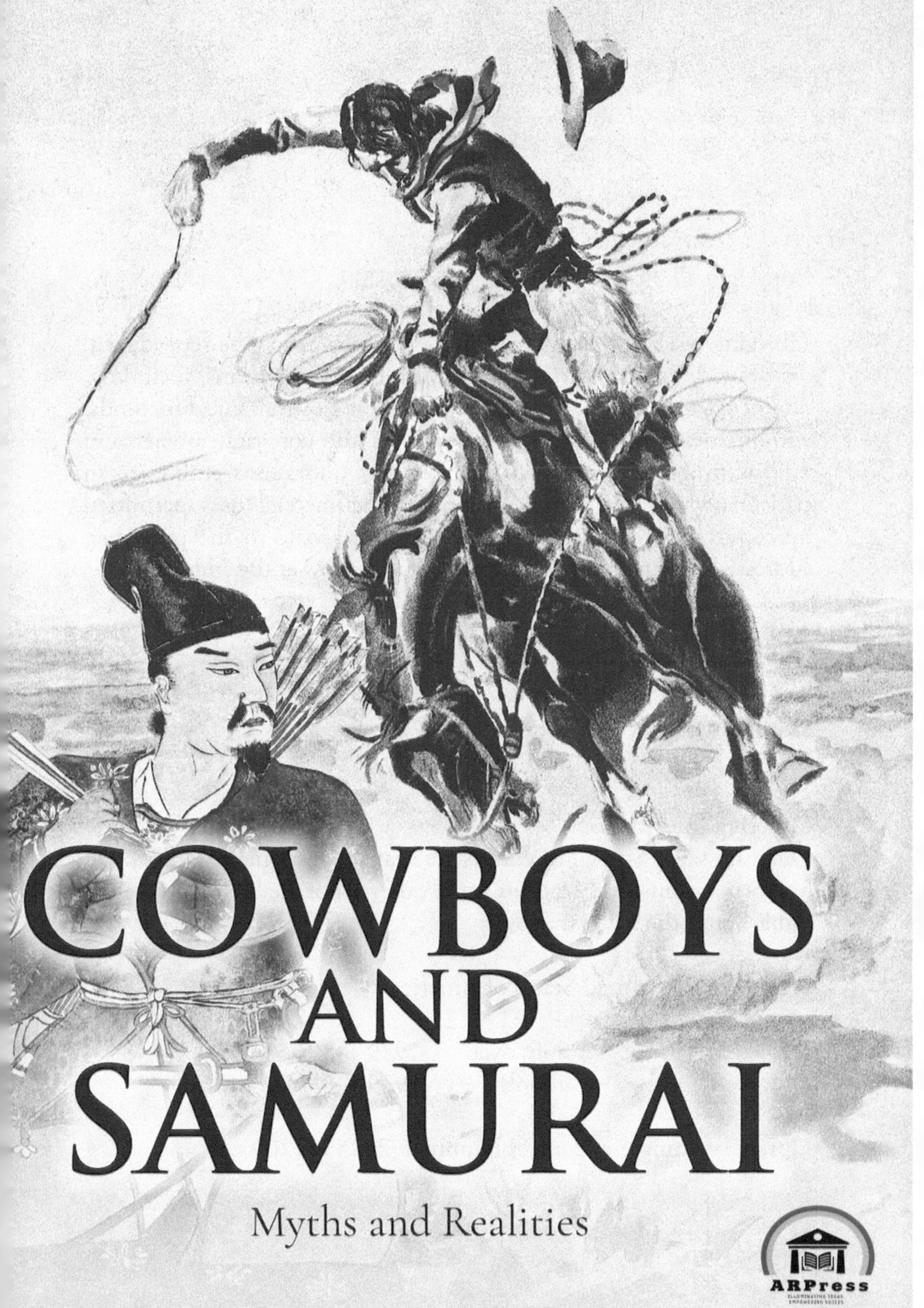

COWBOYS AND SAMURAI

Myths and Realities

ARPress
45 Dan Road Suite 5
Canton MA 02021
Hotline: 1(888) 821-0229
Fax: 1(508) 545-7580

Ordering Information:
Quantity sales. Special discounts are available on quantity purchases by corporations, associations, and others. For details, contact the publisher at the address above.

Printed in the United States of America.

ISBN-13:   Softcover   979-8-89676-047-4
                eBook   979-8-89676-048-1

Library of Congress Control Number: 2025901209

PREFACE

Growing up in the cosmopolitan city of Honolulu in my youthful years, I viewed many cowboy and samurai movies. The samurai films were known as *chambara* (sword fighting). They were my favorite sources of entertainment. It was exciting to see gun and sword fighting with lots of action. The scenes were amazing, and there was never a dull moment.

Those of my generation acquired our image of the cowboy and the samurai through countless matinee viewing of B-Western and low-budget *chambara* films. I assumed there were some truths in these films, but the lack of substance was of no concern since this was pure entertainment. Unfortunately, if not corrected, these images remain stereotypes of the cowboy and the samurai. Notions are based on myths that were contrived and exaggerated. Images were firmly embedded in our minds and were difficult to dislodge. While at the university, I took courses in Japanese history and learned about the realities of samurai life and culture. To my surprise, the real samurai was more interesting than the mythical samurai. When I moved to Tucson, Arizona, and learned more about the cowboy, again to my surprise, I found the real cowboy fascinating. For both the samurai and the cowboy, the real-life portrayals were more captivating than the stereotypes presented by each myth. But the myths piqued my initial interest. And for that, they served an important function.

This book deals mainly with the myths of the cowboys and samurai and contrasts these myths with real-life experiences. The cowboys and samurai are two distinct and vastly divergent groups arising from very different historical and cultural backgrounds. They differ in size, the duration of their existence, and their historical roles and contributions. How can they be compared or even mentioned together? Is it not better to examine them in separate volumes? Here, an analogy is useful. Suppose you are comparing apples to pumpkins, where one is a small fruit and the other is a large fruit. Their colors and shapes are different, and they taste different. In many respects, they are dissimilar. Then, they are cut and blended into a sauce. Each sauce is poured into a crust-lined pie plate and then baked, and presto—you have an apple pie and a pumpkin pie. The process, transformation, and final product can be analyzed and compared. We can examine the historical cowboy and samurai, see what mythologizing, revising, and application took place, and then draw comparisons. Finally, the products can be discussed, as they exist today.

The categorization of the cowboy offered by Professor Joe B. Frantz and Julian Ernest Choate, Jr. is useful for this book. According to the professors, the cowboy exists on three levels: historical, fictional, and folklore.[1] At the historical level, the cowboy has prevailed for about twenty-five years. When the realities of cowboy life are discussed, this is the level we are looking at. The second level, the fictional cowboy, was created by writers, artists, and cartoonists, and on a more massive scale, by performers and producers of radio, movie, and television productions. The third level is the folklore cowboy, otherwise known as the mythical cowboy. Fortunately, the categorization is also applicable to the samurai—the samurai has its historical, fictional, and mythical levels. During my youth, I was fascinated and preoccupied by the mythical cowboy and samurai. They were folk heroes, but reading and studying the cowboy and samurai led me back to the historical figures.

So, what are these myths that seem to capture the interest and imagination of people all over the world? There are several types of myths. Many of the earliest myths dealt with the creation of earth, the wonders of the universe, and the origin of humans. They are called creation myths. Other myths explain natural phenomena such as

---

1   Joe B. Frantz and Julian Ernest Choate, Jr., *The American Cowboy: The Myth and the Reality* (Norman, OK: University of Oklahoma Press, 1955), 15.

lightning, floods, and earthquakes. According to these myths, natural forces and happenings are controlled by gods and goddesses. There was a need for an explanation to give a sense of order and meaning to what otherwise would seem chaotic. This book, however, is not concerned with creation and cosmological questions or questions about the origins of the physical surroundings. Instead, it focuses on the myths of two distinct groups, cowboys and samurai, and their respective societies. An approach, the historical-cultural, is relevant for our purposes because it is involved with myths pertaining to people and their culture. It is from the persona of heroes that certain beliefs, ideals, and values, such as loyalty, honor, frugality, stoicism, and individualism, are developed and become characteristics of the mythical cowboy and samurai. These abstract ideals and values not only affect human behavior, but they also play a larger role in ensuring the continuity and stability of society. Furthermore, myths reveal more than the nature of human behavior. We learn about the cultural setting, and how clothing, songs, poetry, art, and recreational activities were developed, promoted, and maintained. In other words, by examining the cowboy and samurai myths, we gain a better understanding of how certain ideals and images excited and sustained Americans and the Japanese.

With this purpose in mind, the book begins with a chapter on the functions and roles of myths. Myth provides a model for social behavior; thus, it is an instrument for social control. A lifestyle is developed, and a pattern of attitudes and predispositions is created. In the two cultures that are our concern, these ideals and values came to characterize the cultures. Unwritten codes or creeds became prescriptions or guidance that governed the attitudes and behavior of the cowboys and samurai.

Charismatic individuals and heroes were often revered. There is a human need to have heroic and authoritative individuals imbued with high ideals and principles to relieve or eliminate the surrounding chaos. Some samurai were given high accolades, but only a select few were deified or came close to it. None of the cowboys were accorded such adoration, but two US presidents, Washington and Lincoln, were revered and deified, and we need to examine them to see what could happen when heroes are given such reverence. There were no heroes among the historical cowboys, necessitating the need for fictional cowboy heroes to fill the void. Although no fictionalized cowboy hero reached a high level of deification, the cowboy myth has been glorified to such an extent that no North American folklore hero, other than Washington and Lincoln, could match the mythical cowboy.

Part I is devoted to cowboys. It begins with Chapter Two on the origin and early development of the cowboy myth. Here, a historical review is necessary to see how the myths developed. The story begins with magazine articles and pulp fiction that first introduce the life and adventures of the cowboys. This ephemeral literature was soon superseded by more substantive novels but in the same format and tropes. Much more impactful at the turn of the century was the Wild West show of William "Buffalo Bill" Cody. Americans were mesmerized by its pageantry, natives in their colorful costumes, and cowboys demonstrating their horsemanship and roping skills. The introduction of silent Western movies, also had a tremendous effect on myth-making. It began in the early 1900s and reached its peak in 1925. And an even more dramatic innovation took place when the "talkies" (sound movies) appeared. The movie industry became the biggest conveyor of the cowboy myth. This period, right before World War II, was the heyday of Western movies and the glorification of the cowboy. It was followed, two decades later, by a fundamental change in the image of the cowboy and its heroes, a move away from the romantic portrayal to a realistic, unpretentious portrayal of the cowboy hero. These alterations brought the cowboy closer to what he was like. A comparison needs to be made between the mythical cowboy and the real historical cowboy to see exactly what changes were made. Over the years, some mythical images have disappeared, others have been diminished, and are no longer in vogue; nevertheless, they are all of interest from a historical perspective and give us an understanding of the changes that took place.

Chapter Three compares specific myths to the realities of the cowboy's persona and culture. Some myths are misleading, others are half-true, but all are to some degree exaggerated and distorted. Six myths about the nature of the cowboys were chosen to compare with reality. The first two myths deal with the false notion that cowboys are a uniquely American phenomenon and primarily involved white men. The next two myths are about the images of the cowboys continually fighting with the Native Americans and their reputed skills as gunfighters. The final two myths cover the assumed adventurous and glamorous life of the cowboys and the contention that cowboys were virtuous, honest, and practical individuals.

Concerning the cowboy culture, a major omission is the contribution of the Mexican *vaqueros*. Cowboy culture originated from the *vaqueros*. In Spanish, *vaquero* means "cow or cattle worker." Cattle and horses were introduced to North America in the sixteenth century by the Spaniards. The cattle proliferated rapidly, and there was an urgent need to control the herd. Workers hired to handle the cattle did it by riding on horseback, and they developed skills and techniques in controlling cattle. They were known as *vaqueros*. This happened two centuries before the appearance of the American cowboy. Besides the *vaqueros*, other historical advancements helped explain this particular culture. What we know today as the cowboy culture evolved during the cattle drives that began in the 1860s and lasted until the 1880s. The produced cowboy myth covered not only his character and temperament but also the accoutrements associated with his work, including his "trusted" horse, six-shooter, lasso, hat, boots, and the rest of the outfit. While the mythical cowboy was developing, the real cowboys were drastically impacted by technological advancements in the Great Plains. The expanding railroad system ended the need for cattle drives, and since this was the principal employment source of the cowboys, it meant the demise of the cowboys. The historic cowboy disappeared, and only its culture was left. Good or bad, the old cowboy culture has influenced our thinking, and its ideals and values have become part of American culture. For a few decades, the classic and mythical cowboy gained in popularity and became the "real" cowboy, but the stereotype had pulled away from reality and the historic cowboy. However, an increased aversion to this traditional cowboy myth in the postwar period led to the drastic transformation of the cowboy image, bringing it closer to reality. Still, even with these changes, the cowboy culture and its ideals and values have persisted.

Part II moves on to the samurai. The same format from Chapter Two is employed in Chapter Four for the feudal samurai The first section covers the origin and early stages of the samurai myth. Since the historical existence of the samurai was about nine centuries longer than the cowboys, the background information on the samurai is much more extensive and detailed.

The samurai in the early days was strictly a warrior, and numerous legends originated from his exploits, especially the battles fought with competing clans and domains. The paraphernalia used by the samurai is part of the myth, in particular, the sword holds much symbolism. Five myths pertaining to the early samurai were selected for comparison purposes. Two of the myths dealt with samurai virtues, one on loyalty and the other on honor. The other three myths were about the functional roles of the samurai—his fighting or cultural roles, his association with the sword, and the outlier role of ninja warriors.

The next section covers the myths emanating from human relationships and the resulting culture. Many stories dealt with the virtues of loyalty and placing honor above life. These and other virtues are part of the samurai code of behavior known as Bushido. They are embedded in the samurai myths and have permeated the literature and the arts.

Up to this point, the discussion has covered the classical samurai but now the focus moves to the modern samurai. Here, the Western intrusion played a major role in the transformation of the samurai image. Foreign influences accelerated changes in the thinking and response of the Meiji leaders. Two myths are posed, one arguing the samurai is an idealist and the other depicting the samurai as a pragmatist. Both myths are half-truths. There were contradictions, but the ability of the Meiji leadership to work with these differences proved to be the key to their success. It was a departure from the myth when warriors became bureaucrats and entrepreneurs. Some were unable to make the transition and became dissidents. The resulting samurai rebellion ended when the Meiji government's European-style conscript army defeated the rebel samurai army. In the ensuing debate, there was agreement among the leaders that Japan had to immediately become modern and strong, and they could only achieve this by following the model of the Western powers. But, at the same time, Japanese values and traditions were necessary to keep the nation unified. Meiji myth-makers deftly combined innovations of the West with the virtues of the samurai. Modernization was undertaken while maintaining samurai ideals.

Despite the changes, the traditional myth has a lasting impact on Japanese culture. This is the legacy of the samurai myth. Some of the samurai values and ideals continued and have colored present-day Japanese thinking. The influence is there and is part of Japanese culture.

The book ends with an epilogue—a discussion about the impact of the revised myths of the cowboys and samurai on contemporary culture and society. Myth is a two-edged sword. It could be a unifying force, providing the nation with positive purposes, a national identity, and patriotism. On the other hand, it could be a divisive force serving malevolent purposes. It could lead to tough-minded relationships with other countries. Whatever the objectives, cowboy and samurai myths play similar roles. Although cowboy and samurai cultures are widely separate and distinct, they have influenced and borrowed from each other. Whether these values and ideals have an international or universal impact is problematic.

Since the book is for the general reader, a few comments about the Japanese and Spanish languages. Japanese names are in the Japanese style, with the family name first, followed by the given name. Japanese sources, whether written or spoken, use the traditional Japanese style. However, there are exceptions. The names of Japanese authors and film directors whose works are available in English are given in the Western style, for example, Akira Kurosawa (films are available in English) and Yukio Mishima (writings are available in translation). Although names of old historical figures are always given in the Japanese style, names of famous modern-era historical figures are rendered in the Western style because this is how they are cited in most English texts. Saigo Takemori, for example, is usually written in the Western style with the given name first. I decided to follow this practice so as not to confuse the reader. Some Japanese have different names, so I chose the one most frequently used. A glossary is provided to help decipher the many Japanese words and a few Spanish words employed in the text. Besides the definition, appropriate background information is included. Japanese, Spanish, and other foreign words are italicized, except for names of places, personal names, and words accepted into the English language and listed in Merriam-Webster's Collegiate Dictionary, Eleventh Edition. Singular and plural are not distinguished in Japanese, so the English plural "s" is not used. Samurai could mean a single samurai or several samurai, depending on the context. To simplify matters, the macron, a diacritical mark placed above a vowel, indicating a stressed and elongated vowel, has been omitted from Japanese words.

Acknowledgments

Journalists, scholars, and other writers have written extensively about the cowboys and samurai. Collections of fables, legends, stories, letters, diaries, documents, and works of arts, including songs and poetry have been examined with their commentaries. The literature is voluminous. As a result, we have a reasonable picture of what life was like in the days of the cowboys and samurai. I am indebted to these researchers.

In the preparation of the manuscript, I had the support of my family. Evelyn, my partner, gave continual support for the endeavor. My daughter Lisa, edited the manuscript, correcting errors and making the text more readable, and my son, Mark, helped with computer questions.

CHAPTER ONE

ROLES AND FUNCTIONS OF MYTHS

Myths are found in every culture and have played a part in every civilization. Long before humans preserved their lore, they transmitted the myths by word of mouth. Recording myths is a recent development in the long annals of the human race. Once the stories were written, they became elaborate. These folktales and sagas evolved into legends. They go back in antiquity and have been passed on from generation to generation. Because they are widespread and varied, it is difficult to categorize them. Researchers have created typologies of myths, listing them by functions and structures. But for our purposes, there is no need to debate how to classify myths or to have philosophical discussions on how to treat myths.

At the simplest level, myths can be categorized into three broad types: etiological, psychological, and historical-cultural. Etiological myth is a fancy word for a creation myth. Humans wondered why they exist. Who created the ground they walk on and the sun, moon, and stars? What causes floods, lightning, winds, and other natural phenomena? Why are there deaths and wars? There were no obvious answers to these questions, but explanations were desperately needed. Therefore, stories were made up, and they slowly evolved, providing answers to these perplexing questions.

When people think of myth, they usually refer to the mythology of the Greeks and Romans, which is related to etiological myths. Gods and goddesses are the source or cause for all the natural phenomena and actions. They are the answers to the questions about lightning, storms, earthquakes, and the chaos of life. The most powerful of the twelve Greek deities were Zeus, Poseidon, and Hades, with Zeus having ultimate control over all the gods and goddesses. The deities had multiple tasks, and their duties overlapped, creating a complex mythology.

Elaborate mythology was of no interest and had no relevance to cowboys. Cowboys were fully occupied with the challenges of frontier life, so ethereal matters were unimportant. They were known for their down-to-earth thinking, and their attention was on the immediate surroundings. In their relationships, they employed common sense and avoided the argumentative approach.

In contrast, samurai were indirectly linked with etiological myths. From the beginning, samurai were closely connected to the indigenous Shinto religion with its pantheistic beliefs that supernatural entities called *kami* resided in natural objects such as rocks and trees. They were, in fact, everywhere. In addition, by the seventeenth century, a philosophical movement called Neo-Confucianism became a major influence on the samurai's social relationships and their ethical and moral behavior and thoughts. The impact of Neo-Confucianism can be seen, for example, in Bushido (the way of the warrior), the moral code of the samurai. The contribution of Zen Buddhism is also apparent in Bushido. Therefore, these religious and philosophical movements created links with Japanese etiological myths and are part of the samurai tradition.

As the samurai evolved, the broad etiological myths became secondary to the specific concern with myths associated with the imperial lineage. Early on, the samurai were given the task of serving the emperor, the imperial family, and the court. The earliest recorded writings of ancient Japan are filled with myths, legends, and historical accounts of the imperial line, starting with Jimmu, the legendary first emperor. The lineage was traced back to the creators of the Japanese islands, the god Izanagi and the goddess Izanami to legitimize the imperial family. The Japanese creation myth and the whole body of mythology are more complex than those of the Greeks and Romans.

There are a myriad of deities, and the exploits and tales are numerous. Many of the rituals and traditions mentioned in the writings were incorporated into the Shinto religion. For the practical samurai, these myths were superfluous and had little to do with their principal duty of providing security for the emperor and his court. Only a few clans had close association with the imperial family. In these domains, the samurai's fealty was not only to his feudal lord but extended to the emperor. Nevertheless, in the majority of the domains, the emperor was not given such loyalty. Japanese emperors in the early periods were not considered "sacred and inviolable." Hence, as the samurai progressed, etiological questions played a minor role in the samurai's thinking.

As mentioned earlier, the second way of understanding myths is through the psychological approach. The most prominent proponent is C. G. Jung. For Jung, the mind is not a blank sheet; there are some predispositions. According to Jung, myths are based on human emotions and come from the subconscious mind. Myths are expressions of the collective unconscious. They express core ideas that are part of human beings. Myths express wisdom encoded in all humans; these are called archetypes—general forms and patterns that explain the nature of the world and life and are used by all cultures. An archetype is an inherited idea or mode of thought derived from the cultural experience and present in the unconscious of the individual. Therefore, myths are not about gods or explanations of the physical world. They are about the human mind, which makes the process an inner rather than an outer process.[2]

It does not help in analyzing the cowboys and samurai myths to get into the controversy between the etiological, with its focus on magic and religion, and the psychological explanations of myths. These are two distinct and different approaches. The third approach, the historical-cultural, is better suited for discussing the unique myths that developed within the cowboy and samurai cultures. In the historical-cultural analysis, myths are examined in terms of the nature of society, human relationships, working conditions, and cultural expressions.

Myth can be defined as follows: It is a narrative that uses symbols, imageries, historical events, and other visual means to create popular belief or tradition about certain rituals, individuals, or groups. It instills ideals, values, attitudes, and predispositions. Myth provides

---

2   Robert A. Segal, *Theorizing About Myth* (Amherst, MA: University of Massachusetts Press, 1999), 67-80. For Jung's writings on myths, see Robert A. Segal, ed. *Jung on Mythology* (Princeton, NJ: Princeton University Press, 1998).

an ethical model of proper behavior. As images, they fulfill the need to enliven society by creating excitement and pride. But how do you create popular belief and instill ideals? An obvious way is to elevate certain acts of a group or individual to a heroic level, often based on an actual historical event or a real person, and the treatment tends to be overstated and embellished. It starts with kernels of truth, which are expanded with pure fabrication and fanciful notions. Frequently, the narratives are presented as authoritative factual accounts. These collective representations are commonly known as folklore and legends and become part of the established culture. It was only in the 1830s that the word "myth" began to be widely used, and it had a negative connotation, referring to an unfounded or false body of ideas and stories. Thus, the word "myth" is a relatively recent development and has had to overcome negativity.[3]

The overall myth that is initially developed can be referred to as the "traditional or classical myth," and its life span is determined by historical events. The life span of the traditional myth of the cowboys was short; it only lasted from the 1850s to the 1890s. It was too short for many Americans, who felt the need for a tradition extending back several more years. But there were no castles or knights in America. Somehow, there had to be a unifying narrative extending from the past to the future. The answer was the mythical cowboy. Although limited by the short duration of the historic cowboy, it could be prolonged well into the future. However, as it turned out, domestic and outside forces soon rendered the traditional myth obsolete; it was no longer relevant under changing circumstances. Instead, it was replaced by a modified myth, which no longer served as an overarching influence but provided a way of thinking based on its ideals and values.

By way of contrast, the life span of the traditional samurai myth was much longer. It started in the ninth century and was firmly established by the eleventh century, lasting until 1876, when the samurai class was officially abolished. With the beginning of modernization, the traditional samurai myth was transformed. Parts of the myth were resurrected from time to time for their virtuous features, something to be admired, even in a nostalgic vein. Despite all the changes, the values of the myth continued to influence the thinking of the samurai elites.

---

3   *Merriam-Webster's Collegiate Dictionary,* 11th ed. (Springfield, MA: Merriam-Webster, 2003), 822.

The dissemination of the cowboy and samurai myths in the nineteenth century was dependent on written records—historical chronicles, documents, diaries, literature, poems, lyrics, and so forth. Leading subjects' lifestyles and careers were glamorized. Chosen were the most dramatic stories about the extraordinary exploits and actions of specific individuals, and based on these accounts, they were acclaimed as heroes. The heroic figures provided hope and a sense of pride. They, after all, overcame fear, oppression, and ignorance and brought the community together.[4]

Occasionally, the hero is elevated to divine status in a process known as apotheosis. None of the cowboy heroes, as we know them, achieved such status. Hollywood actors portrayed them, and the actors themselves were not heroes but celebrities. These heroic figures were, of course, fictional—they became the mythical cowboy heroes.

In contrast, many of the samurai heroes were actual historical figures. A small number of samurai warriors came close to being deified, and one became deified. Saigo Takamori, a charismatic and paradoxical leader achieved deification. He rebelled against the government and was killed in what is considered the last stand of the samurai. Although he was on the losing side, Saigo was admired for his courage, loyalty, and sense of honor and duty. He had the right motive—he did it for the sake of his country. Saigo defended the samurai profession against criticisms, and though an admirer of modernization, he opposed its corrupting influence on Japanese ideals and virtues. After his death, artists had him looking down on Japan from heaven and newspaper accounts associated him with celestial bodies. Further details of his deification is given in Chapter Four under the discussion of the myth of the samurai as a killing warrior while at the same time being a cultured warrior.

What happens when apotheosis takes hold? In the US, two presidents, George Washington and Abraham Lincoln, showed what could transpire when apotheosis occurs. For both presidents, the process began with the stories of their youth. Mason Locke Weems, better known as Parson Weems, wrote the fable of the youthful Washington chopping down his father's cherry tree. Washington then confessed to his father that he was guilty with the famous phrase: "I cannot tell a lie." The tale was written in the nineteenth century, and most American schoolchildren learned about it. Grant Wood, the renowned American

---

4   Joseph Campbell, *The Hero with a Thousand Faces*, 3rd ed. (Novato, CA: New World Library, 2008).

painter, elevated Washington's mystique by painting the scene of the chopped cherry tree in 1939 at the height of Nazism and fascism to promote American patriotism. It is interesting to see that Wood painted the adult head of Washington on the youthful Washington. The head of Washington is from Gilbert Stuart's famous portrait of Washington, a picture most Americans would instantly recognize. It is the head profile of Washington that is on the one-dollar bill. The public knows Washington by this portrait and would not accept any other versions—you do not change a deified man. Parson Weems is pointing to the scene on the right side of the painting.

Washington and the cherry tree

Washington and the cherry tree
Standing on the right is Parson Weems, the writer.
Painting by Grant Wood.

Washington was mythicized for his strength. He is purported to have tossed a silver dollar across the Rappahannock River from his boyhood home. Some stories say it was the Potomac River. However, it is impossible to throw a coin that far, and the silver dollar was not minted at that time. Even though they are fanciful, these myths continue to persist.

Yet the myth-makers failed to recognize what historians claim was one of Washington's most extraordinary acts, his rejection of the offer by the Order of Cincinnatus, a group of high-ranking officers, to make him emperor. Furthermore, he refused to continue as president after his second term and transferred the presidency peacefully to John Adams. In refusing to be an emperor or king and establishing a dynasty, Washington saved the republican form of government and American democracy. Indeed, this was a heroic act, but it's never mentioned in the myth or textbooks. In the process of enhancing certain heroic actions, myths can overlook significant contributions and roles played by the hero.

On May 30, 1922, the Lincoln Memorial was officially dedicated in an imposing ceremony. In attendance were a number of notables: President of Tuskegee Institute, Dr. Robert Russa Moton; Chief Justice (and former president) William Howard Taft; President Warren G. Harding; and Abraham Lincoln's son, Robert Todd Lincoln. An estimated fifty thousand Civil War veterans were in the audience. Through the new medium of radio, the ceremony was broadcasted to the nation.[5]

The memorial was designed as a temple and copied after the Parthenon in Athens. As you enter the building and walk towards the central hall, you reach a large open space with a massive statue. It is Lincoln sitting on a throne and looking at you. The sculpture was supervised by Daniel Chester French. It is nineteen feet high and on a pedestal. In the Greek Parthenon, a gigantic statue of Athena, the goddess of wisdom and war, occupied the open area. The Parthenon, a part of the Acropolis, became a temple dedicated to the worship of Athena. The Lincoln Memorial has become a temple to venerate the sixteenth president. It is the apotheosis of Lincoln.

The "temple" symbolized Lincoln's greatest achievement, the Emancipation Proclamation, which ended slavery. When the operatic singer Marian Anderson was denied the use of Constitution Hall by the Daughters of the American Revolution, she gave a concert on April 9, 1939, from the steps of the Lincoln Memorial before a vast audience of seventy-five thousand. When she began to sing "My Country 'Tis of Thee," it touched the hearts of many Americans. Martin Luther King

---

5   It is ironic that the principal speaker, Dr. Robert Russa Moton, was seated in a segregated section for dignitaries.

Jr. gave his famous "I Have a Dream" speech on August 28, 1963, from the front steps before a massive crowd. Following the speech, Anderson sang the spiritual "He's Got the Whole World in His Hands." The "temple" has become hallowed grounds. There is no better place to proclaim one's civil rights and liberties.

The veneration of Lincoln began after his assassination. Martyrdom sometimes leads to deification. Such devotion was immediately evident in the funeral service and in transporting the president's body from Washington, DC, to Springfield, Illinois. Many people lined the route and stood in reverence as the train made its way through cities, towns, and villages. There has never been such an outpouring of grief and reverence in American history.

The apotheosis of Lincoln is documented by the famous albumen print of Stephen James Ferris. It depicts Lincoln ascending into heaven, where Washington meets him and embraces him and is ready to crown him with a wreath. The print was created in 1865, reproduced into postcards, and printed in newspapers and magazines. It had an impact on every sector of American society.

Apotheosis of Lincoln

The apotheosis of Lincoln
Washington welcoming Lincoln to heaven with an embrace and a wreath.
Albumen print by Stephen James Ferris.

It is with Washington's childhood that the myths about his life begin. Similarly, the myths about Lincoln start with his early days. Indeed, they begin with his birthplace. Much of Lincoln's birthplace in Hodgenville, Kentucky, is a fabrication. It is officially known as the Abraham Lincoln Birthplace National Historical Park and is administered by the National Park Service. The birthplace building is a Greek-style temple and within it is the log cabin where Lincoln was supposedly born. It is a replica and not even a good one. The rangers would tell you it is not authentic.[6] Many aspects of Lincoln's life are shrouded in myths, and even his sayings, many of which have become famous, have been mixed in with myths, making it difficult to decipher what is true and what is not. There are numerous conspiracy theories about the assassination; some are fanciful but others have had serious consequences. Sometimes, it is difficult to determine what is factual and what is fabrication. There is so much glorification surrounding heroes like Washington and Lincoln that it can be troublesome. Will Rogers said, "It isn't what we don't know that troubles us; it's what we know that just ain't so."[7]

We are enamored with heroes. In every culture, there is a need for them. As the well-known adage goes: "If you don't have a hero, you have to invent one." For cowboys, there were no real-life individuals who stood out. A few sheriffs were recognized but were not considered cowboys. The easiest sources to find heroes are in literature and in the movies, but these are fictional characters. In the past and even today, we admire these fictional cowboy heroes.

Finding authentic heroes among the samurai was no problem. Warriors were engaged for many years in continual battles, and out of these wars, real idols emerged. But in the seventeenth century, warfare ceased, and the existence of the warrior class became problematic—in this situation, where do you find new heroes? One approach was to take noted samurai who were neglected and overlooked and remanufactured their stories. But an easier step was to take existing ex-samurai who now held responsible government positions, hype up their achievements, and turn them into celebrities. These newly established heroes would have their stories and exploits disseminated in books, magazines, and

6   Edward Steers Jr., *Lincoln Legends: Myths, Hoaxes, and Confabulations Associated with Our Greatest President* (Lexington, KY: The University Press of Kentucky, 2007), 1-13.

7   Myron Marty, "Lincoln Legends: Myths, Hoaxes, and Confabulations Associated with Our Greatest President by Edward Steers Jr." *Journal of the Abraham Lincoln Association* 30, issue 1 (Winter 2009), 74-79.

the press. In addition, their portrait would be rendered in statutes, paintings, and currencies.

On my first trip to Japan, I remember walking around the imperial palace grounds and coming across a huge statue of a samurai on a horse right before Nijubashi, the principal bridge entrance to the Imperial Place. It is a choice location, so this figure had to be a revered hero. I did not know who the samurai was but later learned he was Kusunoki Masashige (1294-1336), a famous warrior of the Kamakura period (1192-1333). It took several centuries before he was recognized as a national hero and was one of the remanufactured heroes of modern times. When Kusunoki was finally acclaimed, this magnificent statue was placed in the most conspicuous location. In this case, a feudal samurai was honored as a hero in modern times and given recognition through a statue.

While teaching at the University of Michigan, I was on the oral exam committee for an MA candidate. A member of the committee, a historian, asked the candidate an intriguing question: "Who is on the Japanese thousand yen bill, and why is he on it?" The thousand yen note is the most used currency. It has to be a famous figure. At that time, Hirobumi Ito was the figure on the currency. Ito, an ex-samurai, is the "father of the Meiji Constitution." He was a member of the *genro,* an elite group of statesmen who were influential advisors. While serving as the resident general of Korea, he was assassinated by a Korean nationalist. Ito was never mythicized.

Myth-makers occasionally omit or ignore the significant contributions of their designated heroes. Sometimes, individuals who should be heroes are not given that recognition. Historians would agree Ito was a major contributor to the modernization of Japan. He helped establish the constitutional system and held key positions in the Meiji government. But Ito was not a charismatic leader and was never popular. His moderate policies lacked dramatic flair. He was a statesman and not a warrior. Moreover, the Japanese love the glamorous and romantic warrior leader. Even a defeated samurai leader was considered a hero if he fought with valor, and if he should die in battle, all the more, he was revered. Nevertheless, the Japanese government had it right. Ito deserved the honor of being on the thousand yen currency. The US honors its heroes in the same way. Washington is on the dollar bill, the most used currency, and Lincoln is on the second most circulated currency.

Heroes are usually individuals, and singular recognition is given, but another role of myths is to present an image of a collective group. This reputation could be good and positive or interpreted by critics as bad and negative. The images presented in myths are often referred to as stereotypes and caricatures. They could foster unity, patriotism, virtuous behavior, and lofty ideals, or they could promote negativity and be damaging. Stereotypes could heighten one's image at the expense of another group or be demeaning, exaggerating the worst characteristics of the group.

The following are stereotypes of the cowboys disseminated by novels, magazine articles, newspapers, poems, lyrics and other forms of writing. Even foreign observers have contributed to the myths. Two positive stereotypes are cited: First, the traditional cowboys was known for his individualism. He was not hemmed in by many rules and regulations and had a full range of personal freedom. He had more opportunities and was willing to take risks. This frontier outlook was characterized by self-reliance and toughness. Second, he was optimistic. He was ordained to succeed if he worked hard. He had a positive disposition, as reflected by the lyric—"where seldom is heard a discouraging word and the skies are not cloudy all day."

On the other hand, there were negative stereotypes of the cowboys. First, he was obsessed with guns and was quick to draw his weapon. He did not say much but let his gun do the talking. What is the legacy of such an image? Today, America ranks number one in gun ownership in the world; it is said there are more guns than citizens. Gunshot death and injury is an overwhelming problem in the US. Furthermore, the cowboy is arrogant and disinterested in other cultures. He considers his way to be the best and there is no need to learn from others. When working abroad, learning the local language, culture, and customs is unnecessary. This type of thinking is described in the political novel *The Ugly American* (1958) by William J. Lederer and Eugene Burdick. Though this is a fictional account, it is based on facts. In one example, a top official isolates himself in his residence and refuses to help the community. The stereotype "Ugly American" became a pejorative and had serious repercussions for American foreign policy and relations. Foreign countries were offended by the arrogant behavior and attitude of Americans.[8]

From the discussion of the roles played by the cowboy and samurai myths, certain functions can be discerned. Myths can be helpful at the personal and collective levels by answering immediate needs and questions. It expresses, enhances, and maintains a belief in the group's ideals, traditions and practices, thus promoting its identity. Hope is offered, and at times, nostalgia is recalled. It codifies the ethos, the guiding principles that safeguard and enforce morality. A hero is provided as a model to be followed. In all, myths glorify the unique characteristics of the group and instill pride. Most importantly, from the collective perspective, myths are created and used for social control and to insure stability, cohesion, and order in a society.

Myths capture some elements of the truth, but their greatest drawback is their narrow view of reality. They leave out essential elements and even worse, create opportunities for misinformation and disinformation. The real world is complex and cannot be reduced to simplistic images without distortions. Nevertheless, understanding the roles and functions of myths helps recognize their contributions and assess their legacies.

---

8   William J. Lederer and Eugene Burdick, *The Ugly American* (New York: W.W. Norton & Company, 1958).

PART I

COWBOYS

Chapter Two

Cowboy Myths

American colonists viewed with wonderment the wilderness that extended far westward from their towns and villages deep into the interior. Not much was known about the natural features of the land and the natives who inhabited it. There were stories brought back from those who ventured into the wilderness. But for most Americans, it was largely an unknown. James Fenimore Cooper, in his series of five historical novels, the Leatherstocking Tales, written between 1823 and 1841, romanticized the struggles of the pioneers with the frontier and with the Native Americans. The natives pictured were so different they were called "savages." His moving stories of frontier life were widely read and were popular even in Europe. They helped to establish the myth of the western wilderness.

The dense forest wilderness with thick vegetation described by Cooper differed from the wide-open frontier that soon became available for settlers during the Civil War. Greater opportunities seemed possible with the vastness of the Great Plains for agricultural purposes and other economic enterprises. Americans began to think about moving to the West. Horace Greeley, a newspaper editor, is purported to have given his friend the advice that became a dictum printed in newspapers: "Go West, young man, go West and grow up with the country."[9]

---

9   Elizabeth Knowles, ed., *The Oxford Dictionary of Quotations. 5th ed.* (New York: Oxford University Press, 1999), 351.

ORIGIN AND DEVELOPMENT

After the Civil War, there was rapid expansion west of the Mississippi River, and people began to migrate in large numbers. Economic opportunities opened up, and the vast grazing land with sufficient water resources was attractive to the cattle industry. Cattle was a food source that was badly needed. When settlers first came to Texas in 1821, wild cattle from Mexico roamed the region. More longhorn cattle were imported from Mexico, and with no restraints, the bovine proliferated rapidly. This began the cattle business, which formed ranches in Texas. The workers who tended the cattle were called cowboys.

There were anecdotal stories about the cowboys from the very beginning. But the mythicizing of the cowboys began with the appearance of the dime novels, aptly named because they cost ten cents and were printed on cheap paper. Some were fictionalized stories based on real people, but the majority were fictional characters. No real-life heroic cowboy was available. The cowboy was performing work most Americans were unfamiliar with, and there was nothing brave about the job. Herein lies the challenge—a hero had to be created. So, the writers used their imagination and made an anonymous cowboy hero. A few years later, a breakthrough came when Clarence Mulford created the fictional character Hopalong Cassidy. Cassidy first appeared in a short story in 1904 and became an archetype heroic cowboy. Acted by William Boyd, Cassidy appeared in many radio, film, and television shows and was featured in comic strips. Boyd appeared in fifty-four B-movies and became wealthy from the royalties and appearance fees. However, few recall William Boyd's name, while Hopalong Cassidy has become world-famous and is remembered.

Hopalong Cassidy (William Boyd) with "Topper"

Then, pulp fiction began to appear in the 1890s. These pulp magazines were called "pulp" because they were printed on cheap wood pulp paper. Racy and full of action, the magazine stories had the usual trope of shoot-outs and damsels in distress. The images portrayed were stereotypes of cowboys, Native Americans, gunfighters, and outlaws. These short stories had little literary value. While the adventures depicted in these stories of the Old West made for interesting reading, they severely deviated from historical reality.

A departure from the dime novels and pulp magazines were works of a more substantive nature that gave an in-depth description of life on the western plains. *The Virginian: A Horseman of the Plains* (1902) by Owen Wister (1860-1938) was the first of this type of novel. Wister was a Harvard Law School graduate, but after several years, gave up the law profession and became a writer. He made six trips to the Wild West and was enamored with the American West like his friend Theodore Roosevelt. Based on his visits, he wrote about the Wyoming Territory between 1874 and 1890 but no mention was made of Texas, where the cowboy originated. What Wister referred to as horseman or cow-puncher was, of course, the cowboy, but his cowboy hero never tended cattle or cows. Moreover, his hero was anonymous, known only as "the Virginian." When he wrote the book, the cowboy and the traditional West were disappearing, and Wister lamented its demise. He set out to endow his cowboy with natural nobility. For him, the cowboy is thoroughly Anglo-Saxon, racially and culturally. He romanticized the cowboy, seeing virtues in the simple, honest, and strenuous life. Depicting violence was not his strong point, but his shoot-out is the first of its kind in a novel.[10]

Owen Wister

The Virginian was widely read and had a large following, but the novels by Zane Grey (1872-1939) were more popular, especially his *Riders of the Purple Sage* (1912). A former dentist turned writer, his adventurous stories about the Wild West—full of action, violence, romance and picturesque landscape—helped to establish the West as a literary genre. Soon other novelists wrote about the Old West but only a very few achieved fame; those that became famous were noted for their abundant output. A contemporary of Grey was the prolific writer

10 Owen Wister, The Virginian: *A Horseman of the Plains* (New York: The Macmillan Company, 1902).

Frederick Schiller Faust, writing under the pseudonym Max Brand (1892-1944). His better-known novels were written in the 1920s. Wister wrote one book, and Grey and Brand wrote many Western novels, but the heroes in their books do not stand out and are relatively unknown. However, their pre-World War II books established the myth of the cowboy culture on the mass level. This line of popular Western novels was continued in the postwar era by another prolific writer, Louis L'Amour (1908-1988). He probably sold more books than any other writer of Westerns. His stories followed the same formula and did not add new substance, but they were popular, and many of his stories were made into films. L'Amour's works are not noted for their literary quality, but the sheer volume made an indelible impression on the myth of the cowboy. He reinforced the myth established by Wister, Grey, and Brand, and this myth, in diluted form, lingers to this day.

Europeans were fascinated by stories of the American West, starting with the early novels about frontier life by James Fenimore Cooper. It is not adequately recognized, but the German writer Karl May wrote several stories on the Old West. His books were widely read and translated, and millions of copies were sold. He wrote his novels after researching and reading whatever books he could find on the Wild West, then used his imagination. He took one trip to America after he wrote his novels, but it was to the East Coast, and he never visited the Old West. May's novels were written at the turn of the century and, together with those of Wister, Grey, and Brand, helped to create the composite image of the fictional cowboy.

A massive breakthrough in the popularization of the cowboy came with the Wild West show of William F. Cody (1846-1917), better known as "Buffalo Bill." Between 1883 and 1906, Buffalo Bill's Wild West show toured the US. In addition, the show was performed before enthusiastic crowds in England, France, Spain, Italy, Germany, and Austria-Hungary between 1887 and 1906. In the US, huge throngs of people attended, and the tours were highly successful. Why were the shows appealing? Cody's extravaganza presented life and culture so different from that of the cities and towns. The vision of vast open space and primitive natives seemed exotic and adventuresome. It stirred and captured the attention of Americans. They were fascinated by the sight of buffalo and Native Americans in their colorful costume, especially the men wearing elaborate headdresses. Stage drama had actors in authentic costumes reenacting historical events. Aging cowboys displayed their roping and trick shots, and Annie Oakley, in her cowgirl outfit, showed remarkable shooting skills. Oakley purportedly shot a cigarette off her husband's mouth! She was not a cowgirl and kept her femininity. But other women performers were real cowgirls. They showed riding skills with the horses, did roping, and a few rode the bucking broncos.

William F. "Buffalo Bill" Cody

Buffalo Bill's Wild West was an enormous production. It had as many as five hundred cast and staff members, which included twenty-five cowboys, a dozen cowgirls, and one hundred Native American men, women, and children. The animal contingent was large, comprising over a hundred show and draft horses and about thirty buffalo. A parade preceded the show in the cities and towns toured by the company. The performance itself took two hours.

Cody was familiar with the Great Plains. He was authentic. His family lived in Iowa and Kansas. He moved around several western states and held different jobs, including being a Pony Express rider, stagecoach driver, buffalo hunter, and serving in the military as a scout.[11] He was also a rancher but not a cowboy. In his show, Cody insisted on authenticity and wanted to portray the true West. But he was a shrewd showman and promoter and knew compromises had to be made to make the show exciting. He demonstrated that one could have authenticity in the entertainment world by combining historical facts with the spectacular. Various forms of publicity were employed to reach the public, ranging from posters to advertisements in tabloid newspapers and magazines.

The influence of Cody was enormous. His show's portrayal of the Old West influenced writers, artists, and people in the movie industry. The harshness of frontier life was displayed, as well as the beauty of its primitive surroundings. The cowboys, noted for living simple lives, were shown to be optimistic and determined, having overcome challenges through strenuous efforts. By employing a large number of Native Americans, Cody made the American public aware of their legitimate needs and aspirations. Still, it did not begin to solve the problems of the indigenous population. He also employed many women, believed in women's rights, and treated women fairly. In the early stages of the Wild West show, there were a few African American employees, but they were gradually laid off. Unfortunately, the myth crystallized that the cowboys were all-white, and this view persisted for a long time. But Cody did recognized the horse-culture groups as being world-wide. In his show, he invited Arabs, Turks, gauchos, and Mongols to display their unique horses and colorful costumes.[12]

In one of the main events of the Wild West show, cowboys demonstrated skills in roping and the various techniques used to capture or control animals. Following the same line of events in the Cody show, a competitive sport called rodeo began in a few communities. The word "rodeo" is derived from the Spanish verb *rodear*, meaning "to surround or roundup." It features contests in calf roping, bronco riding, steer wrestling, and bull riding. Rodeo is not like the Wild West show; it is not an extravaganza, but a series of contests, an athletic event testing the skills of cowboys. The rodeo started much earlier than the

11 Whether Cody was a Pony Express rider is questionable. It is a problem to authenticate the background information on historic and heroic figures. In works on these individuals, and even in primary sources, misinformation has crept in, making it difficult to discern the actual facts from fabrications. Jeremy Agnew, *The Old West in Fact and Film: History Versus Hollywood* (Jefferson NC: McFarland & Company, 2012), 18.
12 For books on the life of Cody, see Joseph G. Rosa and Robin May, *Buffalo Bill and His Wild West: A Pictorial Biography* (Lawrence, KS: University Press of Kansas, 1989); Henry Blackman Sell and Victor Weybright, *Buffalo Bill and the Wild West* (New York: Oxford University Press, 1955).

Wild West show, with the earliest event held on July 4, 1869, in Deer Trail, Colorado. It was followed by rodeos in Cheyenne, Wyoming (1872) and Pecos, Texas (1883). But Cody's show gave impetus to the rodeo and popularized it. The event held in Prescott, Arizona, on July 4, 1888, is recognized as the first official rodeo because it presented prizes. Today, there are rodeos throughout the US, and some feature a parade and a livestock show. Tucson, Arizona will celebrate its one hundred years of rodeo in 2025. The western states with rodeos are Texas, Arizona, Nevada, Wyoming, Colorado, Idaho, Oregon, Washington, California, Utah, New Mexico, and South Dakota. The events continue to promote the myth of the cowboy and its culture, albeit in modified form.

Magazines, novels, the Wild West show, and rodeos all contributed to the image of the cowboy and its culture. The visual arts also added to the build-up of the image. Photography was expanding, but paintings gathered more attention with their vivid hues and composition of Western landscapes, portraits of Native Americans, and cowboys in action. Foremost among the Western artists was Frederic Remington (1861-1909), a noted painter, illustrator, and sculptor. He depicted scenes of the Old West of the 1880s. Remington was not a Westerner, but he was fascinated with the Wild West and admired the rough and stoic cowboys for enduring intolerable conditions. His paintings and drawings of the cowboys on horseback, herding the cattle, and hunting buffalos made an indelible impression.[13] Magazine articles he wrote in the 1880s and 1890s had illustrations of cowboys, soldiers, and Native Americans. These images became the accepted version of how the American public viewed the West. President Theodore Roosevelt, who embodied the cowboy spirit and considered the cowboys his heroes, had a close friendship with the painter. Roosevelt admired Remington's paintings, and this admiration and relationship widened the painter's fame and popularity. Remington produced over three thousand paintings and drawings, including the illustrations for *The Evolution of the Cow-puncher* (1895), a collaborative project with Owen Wister. The publication led to an entire Western cowboy genre of articles, novels, plays, and movies. Interestingly, Remington had a different

---

13 Remington focused on cowboys, horses, and buffalo. An earlier painter, the noted George Catlin, concentrated on the Native American tribes. Alfred Bierstadt, German American artist, was known for his panoramic landscapes. The Hudson River School artists primarily painted western landscapes.

opinion from Wister. Remington's prototype cowboys were Mexicans, but Wister insisted on a change and made them whites.[14]

"A Texas Pony," painting by Frederick Remington

Another prolific painter of the Old West was Charles M. Russell (1864-1926). He differed from Remington and did not associate with luminaries. Instead, he spent most of his life in Great Falls, Montana, away from the art world's mainstream. He painted cowboys, Native Americans, and landscapes. In their details and authenticity, Russell's paintings showed an intimate knowledge of indigenous culture and that of the cowboys. Western movies adopted many of his images, and his paintings inspired several songs.[15] Overall, other painters, such as George Catlin and Alfred Bierstadt, added to the image of the Old West. They went beyond the cowboys and painted the surrounding scenes of Native Americans and the wide-open landscapes, thereby broadening the scope of the cowboy myths.

---

14 Emily Ballew Neff, *The Modern West: American Landscapes, 1890-1950* (New Haven: Yale University Press, 2006), 63.

15 See Ramon F. Adams and Homer E. Britzman, *Charles M. Russell: The Cowboy Artist - A Biography* (Pasadena, CA: Trail's End Publishing, 1948). John Taliaferro, *Charles M. Russell: The Life and Legend of America's Cowboy Artist* (Norman, OK: University of Oklahoma Press, 2003).

"Cattle Drive," painting by Charles M. Russell

However, interest in the Wild West waned as Americans increasingly heard and saw more of the once-mysterious frontier. Although still popular, attendance at the Wild West touring show declined. It had a run of thirty years. But now there was a more serious challenge to the show—the introduction of motion pictures. Americans could watch scenes of the Old West and enjoy Western stories on the silver screen rather than attending an event in an indoor or outdoor arena.

The impact of the movies was gradual. Technology that made moving pictures possible was invented in 1894, and in a few years, the widely-known silent Western, *The Great Train Robbery* (1903), was released. Train robberies were notorious in the Wild West and attracted many attempts because of the valuable cargo carried, especially money. It became a common depiction in Western movies. This initial silent film about a train robbery ran for only twelve minutes but was viewed by many Americans and was a huge success. The film was not the first silent Western, but its legacy is based on its wide audience. The silent movie actually had sound with music provided by a pianist and other background sound effects. Short and simple were the plots, with the good always triumphing over evil. Since there was no dialogue, brief subtitles were used.

The following are some of the notable silent Westerns:

- *The Battle of Elderbush Gulch* (1913) - directed by D.W. Griffith
- *The Squaw Man* (1914) - directed by Cecil B. DeMille
- *The Covered Wagon* (1923) - first big-budget epic Western
- *The Iron Horse* (1924) -directed by John Ford
- *Tumbleweeds* (1925) - starred William S. Hart, the first Western film star
- *The Devil Horse* (1926) - featured Rex, the wonder horse

Out of the silent movies, William S. Hart (1864-1946) emerged as the first Western film hero. He maintained his popularity from the late 1910s to the early 1920s. Hart was knowledgeable about the Wild West and wanted his films to be as authentic as possible. He was a friend of famous lawmen Wyatt Earp and Bat Masterson. His persona was that of a dour, hard-nosed, tough cowboy wearing drab clothes. Another Western silent movie star, although not as renowned as Hart, was Harry Carey. His rugged features and baritone voice were well suited for the Western "talkies." Hart and Carey had large followings in the early Westerns. Buck Jones could be included in this group, appearing in many low-budget Western films. These actors laid the foundation for the fictional cowboy. It was a realistic portrayal of the cowboy without the glamor. The main character had a few flaws, was not flashy, and was known as a straight shooter, an upright person.

William S. Hart

In a few years, the Western movie heroes were joined by Thomas Hezikiah Mix (1880-1940), better known as Tom Mix, a silent movie star who also successfully transitioned into "talkies." Mix changed the image of the cowboy hero. The polished hero was now clean-shaven, wore the famous Stetson ten-gallon white hat, bandanna, sleek denim outfit, boots with heels and spurs, and carried a six-shooter. The hero projected a persona of a thoroughly honest and straightforward person with natural wisdom. These characteristics became essential elements in the classic myth of the cowboy. The flashy, sparkling image of the hero with lots of action became a favorite of Americans. Along with the hero, there was the faithful horse, who was his constant companion. Tom Mix had his beloved horse "Tony," which followed the precedent set by Hart with his brown and white pinto named "Fritz." Fritz became a forerunner of several famous movie horses. Even the fictional hero Hopalong Cassidy had "Topper as his reliable horse. The chosen horse and the trusted revolver were required accoutrement of the cowboy heroes.

Tom Mix and ten-gallon white hat

Mix was a skilled horseman and an expert with firearms. He made close to three hundred films. Unfortunately, most of them are considered lost. He was acknowledged as the "King of Cowboys," and he not only influenced the general public's views towards cowboys but also affected those who followed him in the film industry.

The "talkies" with soundtrack replaced silent films in the late 1920s and gradually impacted the declining interest in the Wild West. At first, the major movie studios did not want to take on Westerns. Smaller studios, with their limited budget, produced low-quality cowboy films. Then, in the late 1930s, the major studios, which included Metro-Goldwyn-Mayer (MGM), Paramount Pictures, 20th Century Fox, RKO, Universal Studios, Columbia Pictures, and United Artists produced a series of Western films. The biggest success was *Stagecoach*, directed by John Ford and starring John Wayne. It changed how movies were made and created an image of the cowboy and its surroundings that lasted for many years.[16]

Another genre of Western movies was the singing cowboy motion pictures. They became popular in the 1930s. One of the most significant

---

16 There are three movie versions of *Stagecoach*. In addition, there is a 1966 remake of the film and a 1986 television version.

successes was *The Singing Cowboy* (1936) featuring Gene Autry (1907-1998). Autry became a popular movie and music recording star. Like all movie cowboy heroes, he was not an actual cowboy, but at least he was born in Texas and lived on a ranch.

The real cowboys sang songs while working on the ranch and during the cattle drives, usually around the campfire. They picked up songs from all parts of the country and blended them into their own. The music industry decided to take advantage of the popularity of the cowboy, which was evident in the Wild West show and Western novels. Many cowboy songs were recorded and sung in early Western films. The first "talkie" featuring a singing cowboy was *In Old Arizona* (1928). It was also the first movie filmed outdoors. With the development of radio in the 1920s, Americans were exposed to more cowboy music. It was through the medium of radio that cowboy songs gained nationwide popularity. Autry had his own radio program, and his fame grew with the cutting of new records.

In 1937, Autry had a feud with Republic Pictures, which produced his cowboy movies. The studio decided to groom a replacement. They chose Leonard Franklin Slye, who appeared in minor roles in several Western films. He was a talented singer of cowboy tunes, and in 1933, he cofounded the musical group Sons of the Pioneers.[17] Slye was rebranded and is known today as Roy Rogers (1911-1998). Rogers appeared in close to ninety films. He had a radio show and, in the 1950s, a television series. In many of these shows, his wife, Dale Evans, appeared as a cowgirl. As a cowboy hero, he had a Golden Palomino horse, "Trigger," and a gun, a .45 caliber single-action Colt revolver.

---

17 There has been a generational replacement of personnel in this musical group. The legendary group was originally a trio but became a five-member group of singers with their instruments. They have maintained their popularity. Their scheduled performances are usually held in music halls and theaters are sold out in advance.

Gene Autry

Roy Rogers in **The Carson City Kid** *(1940)*

Tom Mix was the foremost cowboy hero of the 1920s. Gene Autry succeeded him in the 1930s, and Roy Rogers took over in the 1940s, assuming the title "King of the Cowboys." Together, they projected the image of the hero, both wholesome in appearance and attitude. They were optimistic, practical, honest, generous, courteous, and considerate of women. To summarize, the fictional cowboy heroes who came to epitomize what is known as the traditional, classical cowboy had the following traits: they were in their early thirties, medium in stature, although some were six-footers such as John Wayne, and they were all white.[18] There were two basic types of movie cowboys. First came the hero, who is strong, tough, shy, clean-cut, and a silent man of action, always seeking justice and fighting evil forces. William S. Hart, William Boyd (Hopalong Cassidy), Tom Mix, Gary Cooper, and John Wayne represented this type. The other was the entertaining hero. They were also clean-cut but less physical and less prone to be involved in shoot-outs. Instead, they were musically talented and had other demonstrated skills. Gene Autry and Roy Rogers represented this group, and Buffalo Bill could be included. The heroes in both of these groups were associated with a particular horse. These horses became stars, and although they never said a word, their names are remembered.

Chivalric attitudes made up a good part of the cowboy ethos. Several codes or creeds were developed stating principles and ideal to guide the cowboy. It is a picture of what a true cowboy should look like. These creed and rules encapsulate what is meant by the myth of the cowboy. This is a model that Americans could follow, and it would make a friendlier world. Gene Autry had his own code, and his Cowboy Code of Honor is of interest:

1. The cowboy must never shoot first, hit a smaller man, or take unfair advantage.
2. He must never go back on his word or a trust confided in him.
3. He must always tell the truth.
4. He must be gentle with children, the elderly and animals.
5. He must not advocate or possess racially or religiously intolerant ideas.
6. He must help people in distress.
7. He must be a good worker.

---

18 The real cowboys were smaller in stature and not the he-man John Wayne type portrayed in the movies. A smaller rider meant less strain on the horse.

8. He must keep himself clean in thought, speech, action, and persona habits.

9. He must respect women, parents, and his nation's laws.

10. The cowboy is a patriot.[19]

Regular cowboys followed the examples set by their heroes in their clothing and equipment, but it was not fancy, and they opted for attire appropriate for work on the ranch and on the open range. The outfits were generally uniform. They wore bandannas, brightly colored long-sleeved shirts, blue denim jeans known by its trademark Levi's, leather chaps, high-top cowboy boots with jingling spurs, and a big buckle belt with a holster for the revolver. They wore hats of subdued colors, but not black, which was set aside for the villains. Cowboys carried a standard .45 caliber Colt revolver with a regular handle, whereas the pearl-lined handle was reserved for the heroes.

Cinema had an enormous influence on how domestic and foreign audiences viewed the cowboy and its culture. Foreign audiences, for example, were impressed by what they saw on screen, and it reinforced and expanded what they had read. A friend of ours from Japan visited Tucson, and the first thing he asked was where he could buy the horn of a Texas longhorn. Obviously, he was an admirer of cowboys. He went to Texas, purchased a horn, and shipped it to Japan. An average Japanese home is not large, and I often wondered where he displayed the horn. He also asked to see the O.K. Corral in Tombstone, Arizona, where the infamous gunfight between outlaws and lawmen occurred, a scenario enacted in a few Western films. And he wanted to go to Nashville to hear cowboy music. Cowboy music and its counterpart country music are popular in Japan. Japanese tourists could render a cowboy song that is unfamiliar to many Americans.

We all have a view of what a typical cowboy or cowgirl should look like. Hollywood has its version, and it is part of the cowboy myth. My wife, daughter, and I were extras in *Kidco* (1984), a movie about a young boy and his sisters trying to start a business selling horse manure. It is based on a true story. Our role was that of Japanese tourists, imbued with cowboy culture, visiting a horse ranch. We were attired in gaudy cowboy and cowgirl costumes with hats, kerchiefs, and tourist paraphernalia, minus the revolver. But we each had our horse.

---

19 Bill Reynolds, "Cowboy Codes from Western Heroes." *Western Horseman* (October 4, 2017). westernhorseman.com > culture > out-west.

In one scene, we rode down the Tanque Verde Wash, a dry river bed. If you're going to have an authentic cowboy image, you must be on a horse or have one nearby.

The cowboy hero always had his trusted horse, and he usually had a traveling sidekick, a white-male partner. The masked Lone Ranger, a fictional character made famous on radio and television, had "Silver" as his faithful horse, and his traveling partner was Tonto, a Native American. Tonto and the Lone Ranger had a close relationship. He referred to the Lone Ranger as *kemosabe,* which means "trusty scout" or "faithful friend" in the Potawatomi language. In a departure from the standard myth and following the example of the Lone Ranger, the Cisco Kid was a fictional character, but he was a Mexican *caballero* (cavalier or knight). The Cisco Kid appeared in motion pictures, radio, television and comic books. He had Pancho as his Mexican sidekick. Although the Lone Ranger and the Cisco Kid were fictional characters, and in some ways, a departure from the myth, they were, nevertheless, created traditionally as heroic cowboys fighting injustice.

Lone Ranger (Clayton Moore) with "Silver"

The myth about the cowboy persona was built and passed along through novels, movies, and shows. However, there were other means by which the myth was created. Music tells about the thoughts, emotions, and values considered important. It tells us how the myth was developed, accepted, and incorporated into the culture. The real cowboys passed the time by playing music and singing songs at gatherings at the ranch, in the field, and on the cattle drive. A favorite time was after dinner, sitting around the campfire. The songs shared at this time laid the foundation for the later cowboy and country music.

People confuse cowboy or Western music with hillbilly country music. Country music originated in the Appalachia and is a different genre. Cowboy music developed in Texas and was influenced by the folk music of the people living in the region—Mexicans, Native Americans, Germans, Spaniards, and African Americans. It is a blend of various folk music traditions. Authorship of many cowboy songs is unknown. Some were written by people with no first-hand knowledge of the West. Most songs date from the 1860s to the 1890s. The cowboy song "Home on the Range" was one of those sung at the campfires. It was based on a poem written in 1872 by otolaryngologist Dr. Brewster M. Higley, and David E. Kelley developed the melody. The arrangement underwent several changes, but the version sung today comes from the anthology *Cowboy Songs and Other Frontier Ballads*, compiled by John A. Lomax and first published in 1910. Lomax said he heard the song from a black saloonkeeper who learned it from African American cowboys working on the Chisholm Trail. This version became the classic cowboy song, "Home on the Range:"

Oh, give me a home where the buffalo roam,
Where the deer and the antelope play,
Where seldom is heard a discouraging word
And the skies are not cloudy all day.

Chorus:

Home, home on the range,
Where the deer and the antelope play;
Where seldom is heard a discouraging word
And the skies are not cloudy all day.[20]

The song became the anthem of the American West. It celebrates the wonders of the western prairies. The vastness opens up opportunities, and there is optimism—no discouraging words and few cloudy days—truly an American ideal. In 1933, President Franklin D. Roosevelt claimed it as his favorite song, and it became popular nationwide.

20 John Avery Lomax, ed., *Cowboy Songs and Other Frontier Ballads* (New York: Macmillan, 1922), 39-40.

Kansas proclaimed it as its state song on June 30, 1947. With its popularity spreading, countless singers recorded their renditions.

However, among the idyllic description of the landscape, there is a troublesome use of what is now considered an ethnic slur and a disturbing account of what happened in the westward expansion. The third verse is as follows:

> The red man was pressed from this part of the West
> He's likely no more to return,
> To the banks of Red River where seldom if ever
> Their flickering campfires burn.

The "red man" is an ethnic slur, and although there is recognition of the injustice inflicted by seizing the land of the indigenous people, it does so inadequately. Consequently, the third verse has been omitted in some versions of the song.

The ethos of the cowboy was captured in some of the songs. "Tumbling Tumbleweeds" was written in 1930 amid the Depression, but instead of dwelling on the worsening economic condition, it became a symbol of the cowboy spirit.

> See them tumbling down
> Pledging their love to the ground
> Lonely but free I'll be found
> Drifting along with the tumblin' tumbleweeds
>
> Cares of the past are behind
> Nowhere to go, but I'll find
> Just where the trail will wind
> Drifting along with the tumblin' tumbleweeds
>
> I know when night has gone
> That a new world's born at dawn
> I'll keep rolling along
> Deep in my heart is a song
> Here on the range I belong
> Drifting along with the tumblin' tumbleweeds[21]

---

21 genius.com > The-sons-of-the-pioneers-t...

The song tells of the cowboy's spirit of independence and self-reliance, exemplified by the tumbleweeds.[22] He is unafraid to tackle whatever challenges he faces. The song became famous with the 1935 Gene Autry film of the same title, but it is better known today as the signature song of the Sons of the Pioneers.

"Don't Fence Me In" was initially written as a poem in 1934 by Robert Fletcher. Cole Porter modified it and added music, and the song became popular in the 1940s. Roy Rogers first sang it in the *Hollywood Canteen* (1944). Rogers sang it again the following year in the film *Don't Fence Me In* (1945). The most famous version was recorded in 1944 by Bing Crosby and the Andrews Sisters—over a million copies were sold. A portion of the lyrics is as follows:

> Oh, give me land, lots of land under starry skies above
> Don't fence me in
> Let me ride through the wide open country that I love
> Don't fence me in
> Let me be by myself in the evenin' breeze
> And listen to the murmur of the cottonwood trees
> Send me off forever but I ask you please
> Don't fence me in
>
> Just turn me loose, let me straddle my old saddle
> Underneath the western skies
> On my Cayuse, let me wanderer over yonder
> Till I see the mountains rise
> I want to ride to the ridge where the west commences
> And gaze at the moon till I lose my senses
> And I can't look at hovels and I can't stand fences
> Don't fence me in [23]

The song reflects the ethos, the guiding beliefs of the cowboy to be free and independent. He does not want to be restricted or held back; he wants his freedom and to be just himself. It expresses how he communes with nature and his love for the surroundings.

Cowboy songs had their greatest popularity in the 1930s, being played on the radio and performed in many movies. It was slowly

---

22 Tumbleweeds are prickly thistle plants imported from Europe and are evasive, growing wild on the western plains. The strong winds break them off from their roots and the dry weeds, pushed by the winds, become bundles rolling on the ground.

23 www.lyricfind.com.

overtaken by country music in the 1940s and the new style, Western swing, which was meant more for dancing. The heyday of cowboy music had passed.

REVISION AND DEMYTHOLOGIZATION

As previously discussed, there was an outpouring of Western movies in the 1930s. The period from the late 1930s to the 1960s is called the "golden age of the cowboy movies." Western cinema was one of the most popular movie genres in the United States. In the 1940s and 1950s, about one hundred Westerns were produced annually. They comprised about 45 percent of the total movies produced. The movie industry experienced a drastic drop in film production in the 1960s, yet roughly twenty new Westerns were produced every year.

Leading into the 1940s, the most successful film of this period was John Ford's *Stagecoach* (1939). In this film about a stagecoach journey through dangerous territory, all the basic themes of a traditional Western movie played out. This film became the standard for Westerns, crystalizing the cowboy's image, culture, and environment. Part of the movie was filmed in Monument Valley, Utah. Using beautiful and vast landscapes became a necessary background for Western films. In addition, the use of action and chase scenes became a well-established trope.

During World War II, American cinema was looked upon as a platform to fight fascism and other forms of totalitarianism by extolling the virtues of individualism, freedom, and morality. After the war, this positive and optimistic image of the leader or hero was glorified in literature. In 1949, the Western novel *Shane* by Jack Schaefer epitomized what a cowboy hero should be. He is loyal, strong-willed, does not say much, courteous, responsible, and able to handle himself. However, there are differences between Schaefer's version and the traditional cowboy hero. Schaefer's hero does not carry a gun, although he has shooting skills, and surprisingly a drifter. Despite these differences, the hero would still defend his friend and himself. He might be a stranger and outsider, but he is kind and respectful in his demeanor. In the story, Shane is taken in by a family. They do not know his full name or his background. He is like the Lone Ranger, a stranger but protector who will defend against any villain and seek justice. This theme of a stranger or group coming into a community, maintaining law and order by defending against criminals, and helping to carry out justice, became a theme in several novels and movies. The lone cowboy fighting injustice developed into a classic trope. It is similar to the lone wandering samurai in the Japanese films *Yojimbo* (1961) and *Sanjuro* (1962).

The novel *Shane* was adapted and made into a movie with the same name in 1953. Following the example of *Stagecoach,* the landscape background is stunning with the grandeur of the western plains and mountains. Director George Stevens wanted to show the horrors of violence, so the sound effects were turned up and the victims were wired to jerk violently backwards when shot. This was the beginning of graphic violence in Western movies.

Cinematic heroes were not the only legendary figures of the Wild West. Real-life folk heroes emerged, including James Butler Hickok, better known as "Wild Bill" Hickok. He earned the nickname "Wild Bill" due to his exploits with the Union Army during the Civil War. Although gaining notoriety as a lawman, he was a cattle rustler, gunslinger, showman, and gambler. Hickok died ingloriously as a gambler when he was shot in the back while playing poker.

"Wild Bill" Hickok

Hickok has been portrayed as a hero in several dime novels, films and television shows. While he was involved in several gunfights, his experiences have been exaggerated by writers, producers, and Hickok himself. Hickok claimed he killed numerous gunmen in his career, but the verified number was six or seven.[24] By all accounts, he was a skilled gunfighter and excellent with the pistol. Hickok was acclaimed as a hero by the public because of his charisma. He associated with cowboys, but he was not a classic cowboy, and for a hero, he was definitely nontraditional.

In 1936, *The Plainsman,* starring Gary Cooper as Hickok, portrayed the latter part of Hickok's career and his alleged romance with Calamity Jane (Martha Jane Cannary). It was an embellished version of his career. Seventeen years later, the film *Calamity Jane* (1953) and a subsequent musical with the same title followed the line of Hickok's romance with Calamity Jane. All of these productions helped to elevate Hickok as a hero and promoted a revised image of the American cowboy.

A few decades later, another lawman became a folk hero but was not as renowned as Wild Bill Hickok. Wyatt Earp had a checkered background; that is to say, he was a gambler, buffalo hunter, miner, and brothel owner. His life has been covered in books, movies, and television shows. Each recounting of his story has added facts and more exaggerations. Earp himself is responsible for some of these fictitious tales. The myth-makers have made it difficult to separate facts from fabrications. Earp participated in the famous gunfight at the O.K. Corral in Tombstone, Arizona, with his two brothers and John "Doc" Holliday. It was his only claim to fame. After Tombstone, Earp and his wife moved to San Francisco, so his time in the cattle towns of the Old West was short. It was only after he died in 1929 that he became famous. In 1931, the book *Wyatt Earp, Frontier Marshal* by Stuart N. Lake was published and became a bestseller. It was a flattering biography of Earp. His notoriety as a Western hero grew with each publication and movie about his life. Still, Earp has his distractors, his stories have been criticized and the public perception of his life has fluctuated.[25]

Although Hickok and Earp were lawmen and considered heroes, the cinematic cowboy hero was the dominating image. Gary Cooper

---

24 Joseph G. Rosa, Wild Bill Hickok, *Gunfighter: An Account of Hickok's Gunfights* (Norman, OK: University of Oklahoma Press, 2003), 198.

25 For a critical view of Earp, see Andrew C. Isenberg, *Wyatt Earp: A Vigilante Life* (New York: Hill and Wang, 2013).

portrayed Hickok in the 1930s, but emerges as a classic cowboy hero as he plays the role of an elderly lone lawman defending a town against a gang of killers. This is the central theme of the iconic film *High Noon* (1952) with Cooper portraying a marshal ready to retire. He is challenged with facing a killer he sent to prison but is now released and seeking revenge. Most townspeople, including his wife, advise him to leave and avoid confrontation with the killer and his gang. He decides to stay and tries to gather support from the townspeople, but they are afraid, intimidated, and unwilling to fight the desperadoes. Such timid reactions are a sharp contrast to the manly courage of the aged marshal. Along with the classic trope of a lone hero fighting the evil forces, the film has an innovative slant, giving women an independent role. The marshal's wife, a pacifist, has a moral dilemma. Should she follow her moral principles as a pacifist and leave town, or should she, based on human loyalties, stand by her husband? She decides to stay with her husband. There is a dramatic ending with the wife killing one of the gang members and helping to slay the leader of the gang. In *High Noon,* women are shown in a new active role, a departure from the traditional passive behavior of women in the male-dominated society. Nonetheless, the essential characteristics of the cowboy hero stand out in this film: the one-man action or individualism, the unbending courage, and the resolute spirit to fight for justice.

Gary Cooper in High Noon (1952)

The myth of the traditional cowboy began to slowly erode in the decades from the 1950s to the 1980s. The change could be seen in novels, cinema, and television. Why did it happen? In part, it was a reflection of the changes occurring internationally and in American society. Americans could no longer maintain the parochial cowboy outlook. The Cold War began with the United States in a confrontation with the Soviet Union. There were continued conflicts globally, with American involvement in several of them, especially the Korean War and the Vietnam War. Within the US, there were domestic conflicts with the civil rights movement, protest marches, and demonstrations by ethnic and disadvantaged groups. Racism and social inequalities were significant issues. The political and social changes in America impacted its arts and culture. There were challenges to the traditional image of the benevolent and forthright American hero. It did not fit with the realities of American society.

Meanwhile, the popularity of Westerns was coming to an end. It did not disappear, but few films of this genre were produced. The older generation had lived through decades of Western movies and still accepted the facts and ideals portrayed by these films, but the younger generation questioned these assumptions and believed they were inaccurate, overly romanticized, and lacking cultural relevance.

Changes in the cowboy hero were evident in *True Grit* (1969), starring John Wayne (1907-1979) as the hero helping a young woman track down the murderer of her father. The hero turns out to be quite different. He is a hard-drinking, old-fashioned, one-eyed, out-of-shape US marshal in his sixties. He is slow-moving and hesitates to take action; in other words, he is a stark departure from what you would expect of a hero, an antithesis of the traditional hero. It is a harbinger of changes that would soon occur with the mythical American hero. The movie *True Grit* was remade in 2010. Usually, remakes are not as successful as the original, but in this case, critics agree the remake is better. It is closer to the original source, the novel by Charles Portis, with the same title.

John Wayne in True Grit (1969)

From the beginning, Americans were fascinated by the criminal behavior of certain individuals and gangs. A Robin Hood complex is an individual or group engaging in unlawful activities for the alleged purpose of helping the disaffected by challenging the rich and powerful, but usually, they are only helping themselves. *Butch Cassidy and the Sundance Kid* (1969) tells the story of two desperados trying to evade their pursuers. It is partly based on a true story but is embellished with robberies, wild rides, and battles with posses. It is full of adventures and exactly what Americans want in their stories of heroes or antiheroes. This film fed into the movement to challenge traditional Western movies. It was anti-Western and against the conventional image of the cowboy hero. Along these lines were the books, movies, and television series based on the outlaws Billy the Kid and Jesse James. They became legends because of their daring exploits, including bank and train robberies and gunfights—the violence depicted fell in line with the culture of the Wild West. Over the years, a body of myths developed over these outlaws. Some were factual and others were fabricated. Nevertheless, the myths of these antiheroes grew.

The traditional heroes of the 1930s to 1960s depicted in novels, movies, and television shows were based on the well-established understanding of the cowboys' occupational background. Before long, the blurring of the heroes occurred in their occupational experience.

Some were marshals or sheriffs, and others were ranchers and gunfighters. In more recent novels and films, individuals who could be defined as mavericks or drifters with no established occupations. Heroes came from varied backgrounds, some not even remotely connected with the functions of the cowboys. By the 1970s, the staid myth of the Western hero was no longer in vogue and had been modified—revisionism had taken place.

In retrospect, the image of the cowboy had changed even earlier by the 1960s as fewer Western films were produced. Several Western television shows began and took over in popularity. The peak years for TV Westerns were in the 1960s—its golden years. Outstanding shows included: *Gunsmoke* (1955-1975), *Bonanza* (1959-1973), *Rawhide* (1959-1965), *The Rifleman* (1958-1963), *Have Gun - Will Travel* (1957-1965), and *Cheyenne* (1955-1962). By far, the shows with the longest runs were *Gunsmoke and Bonanza*. They had familiar endings, with the good cowboy heroes triumphing over the evil villains. The gun and saloon fights took place against the background of the frontier town or ranch. When the programs deviated from the norm, they were criticized. For example, *Bonanza* focused on personal quarrels and family matters when the attention should be on the operation of the ranch. However, the move away from gunfights, chase scenes, and cowboy routines and towards an examination of the psyche and persona of the cowboy could not be stopped. This became an increasing trend in the portrayal of the cowboys and was the principal theme in mainstream TV Westerns.

By the end of the 1960s, interest in Western television programs began to decline sharply. Shows were terminated, and the majority had disappeared by the beginning of the 1970s. This decline paralleled the downward trend in the movie industry. Cinematic production fell throughout the 1960s and 1970s, and by the 1980s, Western silver screen was no longer a popular genre. Audiences were tired of cowboys and their shootouts.

In 1954, the renowned Japanese filmmaker Akira Kurosawa produced *Seven Samurai,* a classic film that gained worldwide fame and influence. An American version titled *The Magnificent Seven,* directed by John Sturges, was released in 1960. The story is about a Mexican village terrorized by a gang of bandits. In desperation, the villagers asked a wandering band of seven men to help them. The band succeeds in repelling the bandits, and the village is saved. The heroes of this movie are different from the mythical cowboy heroes—they are gunslingers, drifters, and financially distressed individuals. Kurosawa's film changed the image of the samurai heroes. Similarly, the American version altered the image of the esteemed heroes. European film producers took notice.

As interest in Western movies and TV shows declined, a resurgence occurred, but it came from Europe and was a subversion of the cowboy myth. It was known as "spaghetti Western," a subcategory of Westerns that emerged in the mid-1960s. The word "spaghetti" was used because the films were produced in Italy and other European countries. Two outstanding directors, Sergio Leone and Sergio Corbucci, were Italians. This subcategory of low-budget movies first gained prominence in 1964 and lasted for about a decade, fading in the early 1970s.[26] Over six hundred spaghetti Westerns were produced, mostly in European countries. In Japan, they were known as "macaroni western."

The spaghetti style was defined by Sergio Leone's "Dollars Trilogy" (1964-1966). The trilogy began with the widely-known *A Fistful of Dollars* (1964). Leone borrowed the plot of *Yojimbo* (1961), a Japanese film by Kurosawa, and essentially reworked *Yojimbo*.[27] Toshiro Mifune played the principal role as the wandering drifter in *Yojimbo*, and Clint Eastwood had a corresponding role as the drifter in *A Fistful of Dollars*. The characters played by Mifune and Eastwood are strikingly similar; both have dirty and unkempt looks and behave in a surly manner. Mifune was already famous, but Eastwood became a movie star because of his role. The second in the series was *For a Few Dollars More* (1965), followed by the last of the series, *The Good, the Bad and the Ugly* (1966). Two years later, Leone made what critics consider his best film, *Once Upon a Time in the West* (1968). Meanwhile, Sergio Corbucci subverted traditional tropes in *Django* (1966) and *The Great Silence* (1968) using a gunslinger turned monk, a mute protagonist, snow-covered landscapes, and a sad and bleak tone. These two films are considered Corbucci's foremost films and, together with Leone's films, profoundly impacted the cowboy myth.

---

26 See Christopher Frayling, Spaghetti Westerns: *Cowboys and Europeans from Karl May to Sergio Leone*, 2nd ed. (New York: I.B. Tauris & Co. Ltd., 2006).

27 A case of borrowing is *Requiem for a Gringo* (1968) which shows several similarities to the well-known Japanese film *Harakiri* by Masaki Kobayashi. Also *Yojimbo* is said to have inspired *Django*.

In all these revisionist Westerns, the hero is an erstwhile outlaw, drifter, or former gunman. Eastwood acts as a nameless wanderer who plays off two rival gangs and saves the town, but he makes money doing this. It is questionable and selfish morals, a divergence from the impeccable morals shown by the early cowboy heroes. What we have now is moral ambiguity. Furthermore, Eastwood presents a persona different from that of John Wayne and the heroes of early Westerns. Eastwood wears the smallest nondescript hat and is a poncho-clad, cigar-chewing, unshaven gunfighter. Close-ups of him show him sweaty and grimy with a wrinkled sunburnt face. He is always squint-eyed, and in stare-downs, he does not have to say a word; you know what he is thinking.

Clint Eastwood in A Fistful of Dollars (1964)

Eastwood resembled the Marlboro Man, the image of a rugged, individualistic cowboy with a weather-beaten face that was used in 1954 to overcome the image of the filtered cigarette, which at that time was considered a feminine cigarette. The tobacco company wanted to make the Marlboro brand a men's cigarette by using the cowboy image. In late 1963, the new theme of Marlboro Country was started. Real cowboys were used for the ads. It was the time the spaghetti Westerns were gaining popularity. Perhaps it was coincidental, but this emphasis on manliness led to a splurge in the sale of men's products. Not only cigarettes but also men's cologne and toiletries were widely advertised. Ralph Lauren pushed the cologne "Chaps" by highlighting its manly qualities. "Chaps," of course, referred to the leather leggings worn by cowboys.

Another difference from the traditional Western was the degree of violence in the spaghetti Western. The fight scenes were brutal. They were exaggerated and glorified—men were shot with blood gushing everywhere. Whereas in the early cowboy cinema, the shootouts were carefully choreographed with victims slowly falling down and no blood. Overall, the spaghetti Westerns were noted for their realism; in that respect, they were closer to the truth.

Spaghetti Westerns were often described as having eschewed, criticized, or even demythologized traditional Westerns, but they were still considered a part of the Western mold. As expected, the familiar desert landscapes, shanty towns, saloons, jails, horse chases, and bank robberies were present, and the stories had basic happy endings. Some aspects of the persona remained the same, including the heroes' individuality and how they were driven by their sense of morality, even though it was perverted. They had some of the same trappings, and their outfits were the same, although drab. Traditional images did not completely disappear; they were revised, and it was inevitable that the films reflected the drastic changes taking place domestically and internationally. The spaghetti Western dominated the scene from 1964 to 1968, and by 1980, even though hundreds of films had been produced, it soon faded, and today, they are rarely seen.

The revisionist movement continued through the 1980s and into the twenty-first century. In the literary field, the biggest impact on the image of the cowboy and its culture came with the publication of *Lonesome Dove* (1985). It was written by Larry McMurtry (1936-2021), a prolific writer who wrote over forty books, most of which were Western novels. *Lonesome Dove* was the first published book in the *Lonesome Dove* tetralogy, a four-book set. It is considered his best work based on popularity and critics' reviews and was made into a television miniseries in 1989. *Lonesome Dove*, the fictitious name of a town in Texas, is about life in the cattle industry and the ordeals faced by the cowboys on a cattle drive in the late 1870s. There is some resemblance to the lives of the prominent Texas cattle drovers Charles Goodnight and Oliver Loving, but McMurtry said it was coincidental. He debunked the myth of the cowboy as a free, romantic adventurer and optimistic individual. Instead, he pictured the cowboy's life as cruel, brutal, and short, a far cry from the earlier romantic cowboy stories. His description is authentic and gives the reader an accurate picture of frontier life.

Larry McMurtry

There were other authors who countered the American idealization of the cowboys. These novels were considered Western because the setting was in some Western states, and the protagonists were cowboys or characters involved in activities usually associated with cowboys. The events recounted occurred in the postwar period after 1945. Novels by Cormac McCarthy are in this category. His "Border Trilogy" consisted of *All the Pretty Horses* (1992), *The Crossing* (1994), and *Cities of the Plain* (1998). *All the Pretty Horses* was made into a movie in 2000. The protagonists in the stories are two young cowboys. Their adventures take place near the border of Mexico. Even though these works do not follow the tropes of the typical cowboy Westerns, they are important for their impact on the ideal picture of the American cowboy. There is the seeking of adventure and usual attachment to their horses, but the stories have no happy endings. The works of McMurtry and McCarthy confirmed that changes had indelibly occurred in the myth of the cowboy.

Only a few Western movies were produced in the 1990s, and occasionally, they were provocative revisionist Westerns. One such film was *Unforgiven* (1992), directed by and starring Clint Eastwood. The story begins in a small Wyoming town in 1880. The principal character is an aging gunslinger and known killer, who has retired and become a hog farmer. His adventure begins when he goes after a bounty offer.

Unforgiven, in many ways, undermined the cowboy myth foisted by pre-1950s movies. In this film, there is no clear-cut handsome hero. Instead the protagonist has many weaknesses and is a guilt-ridden and regretful killer. He wears a small brown or gray hat, whereas the hero of the 1950s wore a white hat, in stark contrast to the villain's black hat. The cowboy's life shown is not glamorous and exciting but full of dread and remorse. Morality is not distinctly drawn or a black-and-white matter but one of ambiguity. There is no true hero and no true villain.

The *Unforgiven* had worldwide and lasting appeal. In 2013, the Japanese remade the film using the same title. It starred the veteran actor Ken Watanabe, and the setting was changed to the early Meiji period, but the plot lines closely followed that of the American film. The ex-cowboy was replaced by an ex-samurai, who also sought a bounty. Interestingly, changes occurred with the image of the cowboy hero, and corresponding changes took place with the image of the samurai hero.

Preceding *Unforgiven* by two years was a film that created a stir, the iconic *Dances with Wolves* (1990). Written by Michael Blake, Kevin Costner starred, directed, and produced the film. Up to this point, the majority of Western movies had treated the Native Americans as villains or a continual frontier menace. Earlier accounts had pictured them as "savages" that had to be eliminated. Occasionally, they were viewed as friendly and cooperative and used as scouts by cavalry units and government expeditions. Some even served as traveling companions. Buffalo Bill had a positive view of the Native Americans and featured them in his show. However, many held to the saying: "a good Indian is a dead Indian." The racial put-downs were held by many Americans. As a child, I remember the ditty that went as follows:

> Heigh-ho Silver run away
> Tonto lost his underwear
> Tonto said me no care
> Heigh-ho Silver run away

Dances with Wolves is about Lieutenant John Dunbar of the Union Army, who travels to the frontier and is assigned to a remote outpost with a traveling companion. They find the outpost deserted. Dunbar's companion is killed while trying to get help, and the officer finds himself alone. He soon becomes friends with his neighboring Sioux and begins to respect and appreciate their culture and lifestyle.[28] He learns the Lakota language and is accepted into the tribe. There are several incidents where Dunbar protects the tribe from attacks as the US Army pursues the Sioux. The cavalry is also after Dunbar for desertion. Ultimately, he decides to leave since his presence endangers the tribe. In the epilogue, the fate of the Sioux is revealed—thirteen years later, the last Sioux surrenders and their culture is diminished.

Kevin Costner in Dances with Wolves (1990)

The film was a commercial success, won many major awards, and was highly acclaimed by critics. It is a fictitious story, but some characters are taken from the real world. The movie reflects the actual customs and culture of the Sioux and is respectful of the Native Americans, which is a departure from the usual Westerns. But there are historical inaccuracies. The Sioux were not always peace-loving and

28 The Sioux Nation is an alliance of several Plains tribes. Specifically, the film is about the Lakota, one of the alliance tribes. The film has broader implications than the Lakota, so I have used the name Sioux.

high-minded. Contrary to the film's message, the Sioux culture was not diminished. The tribe lives on today with a strong and active culture. Blake used the Comanche tribe in his book, but the movie used the Sioux instead. Two reasons were given for the switch. Comanche had a smaller pool to fill leading roles and extras, and the Sioux had the largest herds of buffalo in the region. Sizable herds were essential in many scenes. However, by using a different tribe, more inaccuracies were introduced.

Lasting impressions were made by the movie. Americans were made aware or reminded of the mistreatment of Native Americans by the US government, especially the actions of its army. Nearly three hundred Lakotas were killed by US soldiers in the battle that became the Wounded Knees Massacre. Although the cowboys were not involved in any of the massacres, still, these incidents had an impact on the myth because the mythical cowboy and its culture came to represent the entire Wild West. Costner emerged as a new type of Western hero, a broad-minded leader who represented more than a monolithic white culture but was influenced by the customs and culture of the surrounding indigenous people.

A preliminary summation of the mythic cowboy characteristics was presented in a previous section, but at this juncture, it is appropriate to point out all the basic aspects of the mythical cowboy derived from magazines, novels, radio, television, and cinema to view it within the context of the changing times. What emerged initially was a myth of the cowboy and its culture that set the tone, and this image permeated America from the 1920s to the mid-1930s. It was the first of three distinct cowboy images. In the initial classical type, the mythical cowboy wore a white ten-gallon Stetson, bandanna, clean riding outfit with a Western shirt and jeans, big buckle belt with a six-shooter in a holster, and boots with spurs. The cowpoke hero was Anglo-American and clean-shaven, and in his demeanor was strong, bashful, loyal, compassionate, generous, and responsible. He was chivalrous and a rescuer of women in distress. A self-made man, he was individualistic, optimistic, and adventuresome. He was a man of few words, had common sense, and believed in clear-cut morality, an epitome of core American values. This first image of the mythical cowboy has lingered to this day because generations were exposed to many low-budget

Western films and television series that embedded the image into our thinking.

The commercialization of the classical cowboy myth resulted in the second basic type of cowboy image. The hero was clean-cut, suave, and attired in somewhat gaudy outfits. The Western shirt stood out with its embroidered designs and shoulder yokes. He carried a .45 caliber revolver and a guitar, although the guitar was not with him while riding the horse. Skilled in using the revolver, the hero was known for his guitar playing and, especially, his singing. The hero was a gentleman but also courageous and a defender of what is right. Therefore, in the films, he was involved in action scenes and the familiar tropes found in Western cinema. Nonetheless, the singing cowboy was a new phenomenon. Although the persona of the cowboy presented was pure fantasy, the ballads sung carried a message—it recounted the challenges, hardships, and dangers faced by the real cowboys. The image of the singing cowboy was popularized by movies, radio, and later television, and the height of its popularity was from the late 1930s to the early 1950s.

By the 1960s, there were drastic alterations in the image of the cowboy. Changes occurring domestically and internationally impacted the third and final type of cowboy image. Western programs were declining, only a few remained on radio and television. Revisionist novels and motion pictures started to deconstruct the image of the cowboy and its culture. Even foreign perception of the cowboys changed, influenced no doubt by American Westerns of that time. Foreigners found the cowboy to be arrogant, boorish, and self-serving. The image portrayed a bedraggled cowboy who wore a smaller hat or bowler with faded, ragged attire. He was older, had rugged features, was unshaven, drank hard liquor, chewed tobacco, and was prone to vices. Pessimistic in outlook, he had an ambiguous sense of morality. In the films, he was the crusader who corrected injustices and helped the oppressed. By assisting those in distress and combatting the evil elements in the environment, his actions were heroic. If possible, he wanted to make money on the side while doing good deeds, so he often had a hidden agenda while carrying out a task. Ironically, these unholy modifications brought the myth closer to reality. The real cowboy was strong, brave, and helpful but had character flaws. It was not always a pretty picture, but this is how the cowboy looked and acted.

CHAPTER THREE

COWBOY REALITIES

In this chapter, the realities of cowboy life and culture are examined. The characteristics of the cowboy and its surroundings are introduced through specific myths. The myths are stated in bold types and are followed by discussions about how realities agree or disagree with the myth. Various topics are covered, ranging from what constitutes the cowboy, his actions, the paraphernalia and practices associated with him, and his attitudes, feelings, and behavior. Some Americans continue to assume or believe these myths to be true even though they are refuted by facts. It is difficult to displace or erase images embedded through constant exposure to mass media and the socialization process. Nonetheless, the reality is plain to see and helps us better understand what changes took place and how they diverged or converged from the basic facts about the cowboy and its culture.

ORIGIN AND IMAGES

Myth: Cowboy is uniquely American

How truly American is the cowboy? The myth claims the cowboy is a uniquely American development. Cowboys, meaning those who work with cattle and horses, are found in many countries. They are known by other names but do the same type of work and serve similar purposes. There are *gauchos* on the grassy plain of South America east of the Andes and the *llaneros* on the plains of Columbia and Venezuela. Those who work with cattle on the Big Island of Hawai'i are called *paniolo*. The Hawaiian cowboys date from about 1850, when several Mexican *vaqueros* (cowboys) were brought over to teach and help with cattle ranching. Many believe the word *paniolo* is derived from the Spanish word *Español*, meaning Spanish or Spaniard. Others think it's from the Spanish word *panuelo*, the handkerchiefs the *vaqueros* wore.[29] It should be pointed out that even before the American cowboy became prominent, the Hawaiian cowpokes were herding cattle.

Most important were the *vaqueros* of northern Mexico. They were the forerunners of the American cowboys. *Vaca* means cow in Spanish and *ero* means worker. It is said that Americans had trouble pronouncing *vaquero,* so the word was corrupted to "buckaroo." Some believe buckaroo is synonymous with cowboy, but others say there are differences between the two groups. Buckaroos originated from California and extended west of the Rockies and northward into the Great Basin. The cowboys started in Texas and ranged northward. There are differences in their use of words, gear, work culture, and practices. But over time, there has been a mixture of borrowings and changes, and the differences have been muted. Both groups did the same job, handling cattle, and both were derived from the *vaquero*.[30]

Mexican vaquero, painting by Remington

29 *Paniolo* are employees of the Parker Ranch in Waimea in the middle of the Big Island of Hawai'i. Parker Ranch is the second largest ranch in the US next to King Ranch in Texas.
30 Lawrence Clayton, Jim Hoy, and Jerald Underwood, *Vaqueros, Cowboys, and Buckaroos* (Austin, TX: University of Texas Press, 2001, xvi-xvii.

Vaqueros fit our definition of cowboy as they worked primarily with horses and cattle. Horses were introduced in 1519 to New Spain, now central and southern Mexico, by the explorer Hernan Cortes. At about the same time, explorer Gregorio de Villalobos brought several herds of cattle from Spain. The Spaniards learned that horses had the strength and speed to cover large areas and were intelligent animals capable of being trained. Soon, the Spaniards were on horseback and could control and drive cattle.

In the southern part of the western territory known as "Texas," vast grassy plains could accommodate large herds of cattle, making it an ideal place for cattle ranching. The herds of beef cattle multiplied rapidly, and ranching became a thriving enterprise. Livestock provided a much-needed food source, and the hides and tallows were also of value. The heavy demand for beef by easterners made the cattle industry profitable, resulting in higher prices for beef. Cattle bought for four dollars in Texas might sell for sixty dollars in Chicago. There was an immediate need for workers to tend the large herds. In 1860, according to the US Department of Agriculture, the US had a population of about 31.4 million people and 25.6 million cattle, and by 1870, more than 40 million people and 21.6 million cattle. Most of the cattle were in Texas.[31] With such a large number of livestock, the potential for profit was enormous.

Over several years, a distinctive Texas Longhorn hybrid breed was developed. It was called "longhorn" because the horns could measure three to five feet in length. This type of cattle was not suited for dairy purposes but was a good source of beef. For the ranches to be more profitable, beef cattle needed good production traits, like the Longhorns' ability to breed at a young age and to breed quickly after calving.

---

31 J. Frank Dobie, *The Longhorns*. Illustrated by Tom Lea (Austin, TX: University of Texas Press, 2000), ix.

Longhorn cattle

In the aftermath of the Mexican-American War (1846-1848) and the Civil War (1861-1865), a large number of white settlers moved into the Texas territory. A few bought large tracts of land. Most notable was Richard King, who purchased land along the Gulf Coast of south Texas. Eventually, he owed over a million acres of land, and his King Ranch became the largest in America. Texan John Chisum also controlled the largest parcels of land in the US, which extended into New Mexico. However, most landowners had smaller tracts of land. When Spanish owners abandoned their *rancho* (small ranch) and herds because of frequent assaults by bandits, white settlers took over the *ranchos*. These *ranchos* already had working *vaqueros,* who were non-Spaniards; they were predominantly Mexicans, with a few African Americans and Native Americans. Initially, *vaqueros* were considered laborers and had little status, but they were soon recognized for their specialized skills. The *vaqueros* were experts with horses and with the rope. They taught Americans how to tend cattle on horseback and other requirements needed on the ranch. Because the Americans learned and borrowed these skills, we can say the American cowboy originated from the Mexican *vaquero*. Therefore, the first cowboys in North America were indigenous Mexicans, not White Americans. Along with the ranching techniques and practices, the Americans also borrowed the accoutrements, language, and other elements of the *vaquero* culture.[32]

Some of the words used by the *vaquero* have been accepted into English. Rope or lasso is *lazo* in Spanish. Lassos were made in the early nineteenth century from horsehair and leather hides. The word lariat, a long rope with a running noose, comes from the Spanish word *la reata*, "rope." The noose enables it to capture a steer, but there is a lariat without a noose. Therefore, both lariat and lasso can mean rope. By common usage, lasso is most often a verb and lariat a noun. The term "chaps" is derived from the Spanish word *chaparral*. Chaps are leather leggings worn over trousers to protect the rider from nettles and thorns of the chaparral bushes and small trees. Other words commonly used in the cowboy culture that are Spanish or derived from Spanish words include corral, rodeo, and sombrero.

In conclusion, a close examination of the cowboy culture reveals its dependence on the *vaqueros* regarding equipment, techniques, practices, language, and traditions. Even though the cowboy is commonly considered uniquely American and shows strong American characteristics, it is truly multicultural, a hybrid, where the influence of the *vaquero* culture is undeniable.

Myth: Cowboys were all-white

The traditional cowboys were not all-white. As noted previously, other minorities were cowboys from the very beginning. No specific count exists for these racial groups. Experts estimate that in the late nineteenth century, one-third of the cowboys were Mexican *vaquero* or *mestizo* (persons of mixed European and Native American ancestry), and 20-25 percent were African Americans. The total number of cowboys was approximately thirty thousand.[33] There is no official cowboy count, but there are records for the cattle population. Each cattle had a monetary value, and because of their large number, a herd of cattle meant a sizable investment; hence, a count was needed and valuable. Meanwhile, the cowboys' pay was minimal, their numbers were few,

---

32 Jerald Underwood, "The Vaquero," in Lawrence Clayton, *Vaqueros, Cowboys, and Buckaroos* (Austin, TX: University of Texas Press, 2001), 1-66.

33 Since there is no official count of cowboys, researchers have used various means to arrive at an estimate. The estimates range from a low of 12,800 to a high of 40,000 cowboys. See William W. Savage, Jr., *The Cowboy Hero: His Image in American History and Culture* (Norman, OK: University of Oklahoma Press, 1979), 7-9. I have taken the compromise figure of thirty thousand for illustrative purpose.

and they were transitory, so a count was unimportant. If there were thirty thousand cowboys, an estimated one-third were Mexicans, and the higher estimate of 25 percent were African Americans, roughly 58 percent of the cowboys would be non-white. Even if the lower estimate of African Americans is used, 53 percent would be non-white. Although these are approximations, it could be argued that most cowboys were non-whites. We would expect the number of Mexican *vaqueros* to be significant since they were already working on ranches, and many more came over with the expansion of the cattle industry. The number of close to 7,500 African American cowboys is surprising because novels, television shows, Hollywood movies, and even historians made little or no mention of African Americans. Even when they should have been used, they were not; in the early period of the movie industry, all the cowboys were white actors.

Thousands of African Americans had migrated to the West after the Civil War, but this fact was seldom recognized. They moved away from the legacies of slavery and sought new opportunities. African Americans worked various jobs, and ranching was one industry with wide-open opportunities. On the ranch, they did maintenance work and fed the animals, and on cattle drives they tended and helped herd the cattle. After work they participated in campfire sessions, singing and playing musical instruments.

There is limited information about African American cowboys, but one black cowboy achieved fame and appeared in a number of films. At an early age, Bill Pickett (1870-1932) worked as a cowboy on a Texas ranch. He invented the technique of bulldogging, where he jumped from his horse and wrestled the steer to the ground by seizing the horns, twisting the neck, and biting its nose or upper lip. Pickett performed his technique in many rodeos and became famous. Bulldogging evolved into steer wrestling, a regular competitive event in rodeos. Pickett competed in hundreds of rodeos, but to enter these events, he often identified as a Native American and not as an African American.

There's minimal information about black cowboys, but even less about black ranchers. One exception is Daniel Webster Wallace (1860-1939), who was born into slavery but, at an early age, became a black cowboy and eventually a highly successful and respected rancher. A cowboy laborer becoming a ranch owner was rare, and for a black man it was extraordinary. He became a major contributor to his community. By purchasing land, his ranch grew extensively and is operated today by his descendants. His story refutes the myth of an all-white cowboy tradition.[34]

African Americans were active in the Wild West. Many entered military service, and to accommodate the Black Americans, the US Army formed the 10th Cavalry Regiment in 1866, composed primarily of African Americans. Native Americans called the black cavalry troops "buffalo soldiers." It is a popular lore that they used this name because the black soldiers' dark, curly hair resembled a buffalo mane, and they fought like fierce buffalo. Altogether, four all-black regiments were created. Their principal duty was to support the westward expansion by protecting the settlers, building roads and other infrastructure, and guarding the US mail.

The buffalo soldiers were in segregated units, and racial discrimination was a prevalent issue. The term "cowboy" originated in Europe. When it was first used in the American West, Black Americans were referred to as "cow-boys" with the hyphen to emphasize the word "boy." Southerners of the plantation era called Black Americans "boys" to denote their inferior status. Whites performing the same work with cattle were called "cowhands." The term "cow-boy" had a pejorative meaning for African Americans. Only later did "cowboy" become acceptable, and the white cowboy myth became the norm.[35]

African Americans played a significant role in the expansion of the West, but this has not been acknowledged until recently. The revisionist movies and recent novels have included Blacks in the narratives, even though there are few Black heroes. African American historians have begun to write about real historical Black heroes. Since many Blacks were illiterate, there was a paucity of written accounts and documents. Much of the research has to be based on anecdotal evidence.

Mexican Americans faced similar challenges. Again, it is in revisionist films and novels that the Hispanics are given a prominent

---

34 Douglas Hales, "Black Cowboy: Daniel Webster '80 John' Wallace," in *The Cowboy Way: An Exploration of History and Culture,* ed. Paul H. Carlson (Lubbock, TX: Texas Tech University Press, 2000), 33-43.
35 David Dary, *Cowboy Culture: A Saga of Five Centuries* (Lawrence, KS: University Press of Kansas, 1989), 83. The hyphen in "cow-boy" was dropped around 1900 by most writers and became "cowboy."

role. In earlier movies, they were frequently portrayed as bandits, revolutionaries, and on the wrong side in the struggle between good and evil. Sometimes, they were chosen as sidekicks for the white hero, but rarely did they emerge as heroes. Even worse, the studios often had whites playing the role of Mexicans. Native Americans did not fare any better and faced condescending attitudes. In films, they were pictured as bloodthirsty savages, wild warriors, and villains. Little respect or acknowledgement was given to the language, tradition, and culture of the Native Americans.

Serious consequences resulted from the notion of an all-white cowboy myth, resulting in wholesale discrimination of racial minorities. Today, the nostalgia of an all-white cowboy has been used as a defense or rationale for stopping the massive influx of immigrants. White nationalists believe immigrants are threats to the American way, taking jobs away, increasing criminal activities, and polluting American traditions. They advocate for severely limiting immigration and massive deportation of immigrants illegally residing in the US. Although it was never a reality, White nationalists would like to return to the so-called all-white ideal.

Myth: Cowboys constantly clashed with "bad Indians"

A frequently quoted myth in popular histories, fiction, and motion pictures is that the cowboys often fought with the bad Native Americans. This was the prevailing view for many decades. As a child, I remember playing "Cowboys and Indians." At the beginning of the game, sides were chosen—you were either a cowboy or an Indian. Nobody wanted to be an Indian, for he was the bad guy; the cowboy was the good guy. The game began once the sides were selected, and we chased each other. It never occurred to us that this was racial stereotyping or a distortion of the truth. We just played the game.

Native Americans attacking wagon trains and white settlements was a common trope in Western novels, movies, and plays. The finale of the Wild West show featured a spectacular assault on a wagon by Native Americans. The classic Western film *Stagecoach* is about a perilous trip through Indian territory with the continuous threat of attacks by indigenous tribes. *Red River* (1948), directed by Howard Hawks and starring John Wayne, exaggerated the dangers of Native

Americans stealing and killing cattle during the cattle drive. In another epic Western movie, *The Searchers* (1956), again starring John Wayne, tells of a Comanche assault on a white homestead, killing three family members and abducting two girls. It was a trope repeated over and over.

From the time of the earliest colonial settlements in the seventeenth century until the end of the nineteenth century, there were continuous Indian Wars. The conflicts were between settlers and the US government versus the Native Americans over possession of native tribal lands. Disputes with settlers became less common as they were resolved by treaties between specific tribes and the federal government. This meant the tribes were forced to sell or surrender land to the US government. Unfortunately, these treaties were often broken by the government and in the ensuing conflicts, many deaths occurred.

But here, the discussion is on the relationship of the cowboys with the Native Americans, which narrows the timespan from the 1860s to the 1890s. The territory covered is the Old West, extending westward from the Mississippi. In this context, there were relatively few conflicts between cowboys and Native Americans, and it was rare for any deaths to occur. Fighting did happen, but it was between the US Army and the indigenous people. There is no denying there was bloodshed with Native Americans attacking settlers and, in turn, settlers killing natives. But when it came to the cowboys, fighting with Native Americans was rare. A favorite trope of Western films is the ambushing of wagon trains by the natives, which provided action scenes for the movies. Several wagon train massacres did occur, but they took place before the 1860s. They did not involve the cowboys, as this was before the cowboys were fully established as an occupational group. Attacks by natives were not a major concern for the settlers making the journey by wagon trains.

At times, the skirmishes between the Cavalry and the Native Americans ended in bloody massacres. Such violence could not be ignored, and the cowboys were apprehensive about the possibility of an attack by the natives. As much as possible, the cowboys and native tribes tried to avoid conflicts. The cattle drovers on the Chisholm Trail negotiated passage through the Native American territory in Oklahoma by paying a fee. On the other hand, Charles Goodnight and Oliver Loving decided to avoid the Indian territory of Oklahoma entirely by going further west into New Mexico before heading north to Colorado. This became the Goodnight-Loving Trail, which stretched one thousand miles from San Angelo in west Texas to northern Colorado near Denver and into Cheyenne, Wyoming. Taking a devious route meant less possibility of conflicts with Native Americans along the cattle trail.[36] The cattle drivers, however, had to keep a watchful eye to prevent cattle rustling by natives.

There was another ethnic group, the Chinese, who faced severe discrimination but avoided bloody conflicts with white settlers, the federal government, or indigenous tribes. The Chinese immigrants played a significant role in the story of the Old West. Initially, they came for the California Gold Rush in the 1850s, but the finding of surface gold in the river beds soon came to an end. The majority moved inland and found work with railroad construction. Eventually, they settled, opened shops, restaurants, and laundries in many Western towns, and became associated with the cowboys.

In 1986, I was hired as an extra for the Western film *Poker Alice*, which was shot on location in Old Tucson, a film location and theme park west of Tucson, Arizona. The movie featured Elizabeth Taylor and George Hamilton. It is based on a real historical person, Alice Evers, but the story is highly fictionalized. *Poker Alice* takes place in the 1880s and is about two vices of the cowboys: gambling and prostitution. I wore a typical black Chinese coolie outfit, which is a loose-fitting jacket with long sleeves, and it came with a black cap. Luckily, a queue was not required. The queue was a men's hairstyle of that period (Qing Dynasty, 1644-1912). The hair is braided and left dangling at the back of the head. Although I am Japanese and not Chinese, it did not matter to the film studio. After all, as they say—"all Asians look alike."

There was racism in the relationship between the cowboys and the ethnic minorities—Chinese, Mexicans, and Blacks but no open hostilities. Minorities were all hired hands and working under the same conditions. But it was different with the indigenous people. Native Americans were dispossessed of their land, and their livelihood was threatened. It affected their food source, religious practices, and the very essence of their culture. Open fighting with Native Americans was understandable.

---

36 This is not to say there were no attacks. Loving was mortally wounded while on his third cattle drive by a Comanche attack and soon after died. It did not result in prolong fighting.

Myth: Cowboy outfits are uniquely American

How the cowboy appears is an essential part of the myth. Previously, a few items of the cowboys' attire were discussed regarding the borrowed words from the Mexican *vaquero* culture. The myth is half-true. Some items are pure American brands, but others are entirely borrowed. Most of the outfits and accessories are functional and job-related, designed for riding a horse and handling cattle. But Americans have embellished parts of the outfit, and they have become fashion statements.

The hat is probably the most distinctive part of the Western outfit. The Mexican sombrero and the bowler, also known as the derby, were first used by cowboys. They were preferred because they didn't blow off easily by the wind while riding a horse. The sombrero is made of felt or straw and, because of its very wide brim, provides excellent protection from the sun and the rain. However, the wide brim made it ungainly. The bowler, on the other hand, is a British import that was popular among the working classes in nineteenth-century England. It is made of felt and has a small crown. While initially worn by the cowboys, it became the hat of lawmen and outlaws.

The classic cowboy hat, the Stetson ten-gallon, replaced the sombrero and bowler. Tom Mix made it famous in his movies and it became his trademark. Soon, the cowboys began wearing them, becoming part of the traditional cowboy myth. The ten-gallon hat has a high-rounded crown, but the brim is not as wide. The high crown provides insulation, and the wide brim offers shade. The lore is that the hat can hold ten gallons of liquid. A famous Stetson company ad shows a cowboy giving his thirsty horse the last drop of water from the crown of his hat. The name is a misnomer because the hat does not hold ten gallons; it barely holds a gallon. The name is probably derived from the Spanish word *galon,* which means braid, the decorative hatbands around the base of the crown. Some hats had "ten *galanes,*" meaning the number of braids, not the capacity of the hat.

Therefore, it was the silver screen that ushered in the ten-gallon hat. The hat has come to symbolize the rugged spirit of cowboy culture. It has evolved from its purely functional purpose of protecting the cowboy from the harshness of the sun to a fashion statement, and it has been adopted and adapted by movie and country music luminaries.

Prominent public figures, such as presidents Harry Truman, Lyndon B. Johnson, and Ronald Reagan, have added to the Stetson hat's popularity and strengthened its association with cowboy culture.

John Batterson Stetson and his company originated the ten-gallon cowboy hat. In 1865, the original version was nicknamed "Boss of the Plains." It was flat-brimmed and had a high top with a straight-sided crown and rounded corners, but was missing the crease in the crown. It later came in various sizes and colors. The white hat was for the hero, symbolizing purity and honesty. Further adaptations took place, and the brim was curved at the edges on one side or both, and the crown had a shallow or a deep pinch, depending on the style.[37]

Not all cowboys wore ten-gallon hats. The bowler or derby was more popular in the American West than the ten-gallon hat. Lawmen and outlaws avoided the ten-gallon hat and preferred wearing the bowler. A famous photo of Butch Cassidy and the Wild Bunch showed them donning bowlers. On the other hand, the notorious outlaw, Billy the Kid, was known for wearing the derby.

Butch Cassidy and the Wild Bunch

Butch Cassidy and the Wild Bunch
Cassidy is on the front row, right side.

---

37 For illustrations of various cowboy hat styles, see Dary, *Cowboy*, 283.

Non-traditional hats are seen more often in revisionist films. The basic design of the cowboy hat remains the same, with modifications only to the crown and brim. Hats are made out of felt or straw. Felt hats are more expensive but durable and preferred by most cowboys. Straw hats are better during warmer weather as they do not hold the heat, breathe better, and are lighter; however, they are more prone to wear and tear. The hat could be personalized, and you could tell where it came from by looking at the crease or pinch in the crown. Despite all the changes and differences in style, the cowboy hat remains an abiding symbol and myth.

The bandana is a required part of the cowboy's attire. Its origin is unknown but could be traced back to the Middle East and Southern Asia. In the US, the bandana was first seen in the mid-1800s and made out of flour sacks. It is known by several names, including wild rag, kerchief, neckerchief, handkerchief, or scarf. The bandana is a large square piece of cloth in different colors and patterns made of silk, cotton, or other soft fabrics. It is worn by wrapping it twice around the neck and held in place at the front by a square knot. The bandana serves several functions, protecting the wearer's neck from the blazing sun and the cold during winter. The cloth absorbs sweat, and when worn over the mouth and nose, it serves as a mask protecting the face from dust storms, which are frequent in the American West. Bandits used it to cover their faces, hiding their identities while conducting nefarious activities. Hollywood movies have made the use of the bandana famous for this purpose. There are many other applications for the scarf, including a bandage, tourniquet, or sling. Over the years, the necessity of the bandana has not changed. It is a part of the cowboy's persona and, hence, a part of the myth.

The Western shirt is an American innovation, although it has its roots in the *vaqueros*. Shirts of the *vaqueros* are made of silk or light cotton, whereas the Western uses denim, a very durable cloth. Western shirts have long sleeves, dual chest pockets with flaps, and press studs, called snaps, instead of buttons. Snaps do not become tangled in clothes and other items easily and eliminates the need to sew on buttons. But the traditional cowboys of the nineteenth century had to put up with buttons. Snaps were introduced in the 1930s and gave the shirt a distinct look. Another stylistic item that made the shirt distinctive was the use of yokes at the top, front and back, which made the shirt durable and gave it a broad-shoulders appearance. Yokes are shaped pattern piece to provide an extra layer of fabric. The stylized yokes have become a major characteristic. Western shirts of the heroes often became fashion statements. They had pipings and embroidered designs, making them glamorous but serving no functional use.

The Western trousers, called jeans or blue jeans, are made of denim, a heavier, tightly woven cotton fabric, making them suitable for ranch work. Jacob Davis and Levi Strauss conceived the jean. By 1890, Levi Strauss & Co. mass-produced jeans made of a new, more flexible fabric, blue denim, paired with their distinctive copper rivets. Blue jeans became part of the cowboy attire—durable, protective, and comfortable. As added protection from briars and cactus needles, leather chaps or leggings were worn over the jeans.

The riding boots with jingling spurs complete the cowboy outfit. Cowboy boots were inspired by the *vaquero* and the boots used by the US cavalry. They came in two basic styles: western (or classic) and roper. The classic style is a high-top boot with a tall shaft and high heel. The heel is usually over one inch and angled to grip the stirrup and keep the rider from being thrown. The toes are rounded or squared in shape, but later in the 1940s, western boots began to have pointed toes. In contrast, the roper has a short boot shaft with a low, squared-off heel and rounded toes. It is designed for the rider to get off quickly after he has roped cattle. The spurs attached to the boots direct a horse to move a certain way while riding. Cowboys use it to communicate with their horses when carrying out tasks. Spurs do not hurt the horse when used by experienced riders. Hollywood cowboys wore boots with spurs even when strolling through town. It became part of their flashy outfit. In recent times, they have become a fashion accessory.

Although the boots today have elaborate decorative stitching, the basic style of the boot has not changed through the years. Like the bandana, it is a part of the cowboy myth, but no myth is involved with the boots and spurs by itself.

Remington's "American Cowboy"

"American Cowboy," painting by Frederick Remington

HORSES AND GUNS

Besides the outfit of the cowboys, there are other accoutrements to be considered. The horse played an extraordinary role in the life of a cowboy. A special relationship was built between the rider and the horse. Here are three quotes that express the feeling:

"A cowboy is only half a man, the other half is his horse"

"A true cowboy never blames his horses"[38]

"There is no secret so close as that between a rider and his horse"[39]

There is trust and respect in this relationship. If the horse is treated properly, the trusted steed will perform as expected. When mishaps occur, the rider must accept his share of the responsibility.

---

38 southernfactor.com > 10-of-the-best-cow...
39 www.azquotes.com > quotes > topics > c...

Horses were brought to the West by Spanish explorers in the sixteenth century. Native Americans were using the offspring of horses introduced by the Spaniards well before the arrival of white settlers. They found horses were valuable in handling buffalo and cattle. Similar to the Native Americans, the frontier settlers quickly learned to use horses, first in farming and then in ranching. Occasionally, horses escaped from settlers and roamed the countryside as feral animals. Their offspring, known as mustangs (from the Spanish *mestengo*), were captured and "broken" so they could be ridden. This was cheaper than purchasing or raising horses. From these practices, the word "bronc" is derived, which is short for bronco, meaning "rough" or "wild" in Spanish. Today, bronc riding is held in rodeo competitions to see how long a participant can stay on a bucking horse. The wild nature of the horse is used for competition's sake, but at times, horses are not treated properly, creating a negative image.

Americans love horses, and mustangs have become a mythic symbol of freedom and an expression of the vanishing West. In the early 1900s, an estimated two million mustangs roamed the American West, but today, approximately eighty thousand are on federal lands with a government program to protect the herds. In 2004, a biographical Western film, *Hidalgo*, was produced about an American distance rider, Frank Hopkins and his mustang Hidalgo. It is a fictionalized true story. A long-distance race supposedly took place in Arabia in 1891, with Hopkins and Hidalgo winning the race and the prize. He used his winnings to buy mustangs from the government and released them into the countryside. At the end of the film, Hildago is freed to join the mustangs.

Cowboys were skilled riders, and the rider and his horse had an affinity for each other, but other than the hero and his horse, movies paid scant attention to this fact. The horse was the ideal animal to work with cattle. It had the size, speed, and stamina to keep the longhorns under control. Moreover, it was an intelligent animal able to follow the signals given by the rider. There are accounts of the cattle drives and ranch work wherein the cowboys expressed their feelings for their horses. They bonded with their horse to such a degree they found it difficult to say goodbye at the conclusion of the cattle drive.[40]

---

40 Cody Assmann, *History of the West with Sam Payne: Trail to Cheyenne* Cheyenne (self-pub., 2022).

It is an enduring image—the cowboy standing next to his steady steed. The silver screen Western stars had their favorite horses. Here are a few: Tom Mix had Tony; Gene Autry had Champion; Roy Rogers had Trigger; John Wayne had several, including Dollar, Duke, Zip Cochise, and Banner; and James Stewart had Pie. Even the fictional Hopalong Cassidy (William Boyd) had Topper, and the Long Ranger (Clayton Moore) had Silver. The relationship was close and emotional, and the cowboy even talked to his equine friend. The Lone Ranger often said to Silver: "Heigh-ho." The cowboys and their horses are indelibly linked; together, they constitute the mythical image.

Myth: Cowboys were gunfighters and experts with guns

Besides the horse, the other accoutrement that impacted the myth of the cowboy was the gun. Movies and television had the mythical cowboys engaged in continual gunfights. Owen Wister was the first serious novelist to write about the gunfights between the forces of good and evil, and it became a basic theme in Western stories. Writers imagined a dramatic scene where the hero would face his foe in a one-on-one confrontation in the middle of the street. No one would be around. Instead, the townspeople would be hiding behind windows and closed doors. It would be a contest to see who has the fastest draw. Naturally, the hero would win, killing the villain and slowly walking away as the townspeople emerged with wonderment. There are no historical records of such encounters. Gunfights, when they occurred, were chaotic and impulsive events and usually involved more than two individuals. Most victims were shot in the back while playing cards or drinking. Some were ambushed or shot in the back when they were fleeing. The open gunfight between lawmen and outlaws at the O.K. Corral in Tombstone, Arizona, was a rarity. Because it was so unusual, it gained notoriety and entered Western folklore. Today, at tourist spots throughout the West, wide-open shootouts are reenacted, but in reality, if there were any gunfights, they would have been fought behind cover, not out in the open.

The revolver is a short-range weapon. It is possible to hit a target at a distance, but it requires considerable skill. For the long-range, the rifle is the weapon to use, which is why sheriffs usually carried both. Experts will tell you it is difficult to shoot a person on the roof of a building with a pistol. Holding your hands steady while standing still is no easy task, but in some movie chase scenes, the hero on horseback is shown shooting at a distant villain while on a fast gallop. Somehow, the bullet finds its target in the movies.

The cowboy was never a gunfighter, and some did not even possess a gun. Those who carried one used it for self-protection against rattlesnakes, coyotes, bears, and other wild animals while on the trail drive. Their weapons were used to kill predators, not to kill people. They did not pretend be a person noted for speed and skill in handling and firing a gun. Cowboys were young, in their twenties, lacked training, and did not have time to practice. On the other hand, lawmen were skilled with guns, and some bandits were good with firearms, but the cowboys lacked such skills. There are anecdotal stories of cowboys shooting themselves by accident while cleaning or practicing with their guns.

Americans have a love affair with guns. It began in colonial times and during the early days of the frontier. Firearms were necessary to defend against potential attacks by hostile elements. It was common practice to place the rifle over a fireplace mantel in a convenient location and easily accessible should trouble arise—it was the centerpiece of the household. The Second Amendment enshrined "the right of the people to keep and bear arms." Guns became an essential part of American life; it was the beginning of a gun culture. The myth of the cowboys enhanced this attachment. Even if the cowboy did not use the firearms, he had to have it—it was a status symbol, just like the samurai sword. Gun ownership became an inherent right of Americans. For some, it implies self-control and the opportunity to set and pursue goals—shooting them gives pleasure.[41]

Concerns over the prevalence of violence led many Old West communities to enact gun control measures. Cattle town newspapers of the 1880s had articles on proposed gun control. Carrying firearms was said to be a "dangerous practice" and totally unnecessary. Town authorities wanted guns entirely banned. In some towns, visitors were asked to check in their guns with the sheriff and the weapons were returned when they left. But, in general, gun control-type laws were poorly and ineffectively enforced.

41 Abigail A. Kohn, *Shooters: Myths and Realities of America's Gun Cultures* (New York: Oxford University Press, 2004), 10.

There was continued concern about guns. Cattlemen also saw the need for gun control, resulting in a Texas cattle-raising association banning revolvers from the cowboy's belt in 1882. Publications of those days asked cattlemen to unite and enforce the law against carrying weapons.

Presently, gun control remains a controversial topic in America, and the same arguments are given. It has become a national political issue and adds to the polarization of the nation. Advocates for gun control cite the increasing number of deaths from gun violence. In contrast, those against gun control continue to cite the Second Amendment and the freedom guns give them to exercise their rights—the right of expression and self-defense. This freedom is subsumed under the concept of rugged individualism, a major characteristic of the mythical cowboy.

Part of the problem with guns is due to the exaggerated picture of violence in the Old West created by writers, artists, and producers of movies and television series. As previously discussed, there were few gunfights, and even though unevenly enforced, many frontier towns had strict laws against carrying weapons. How serious was gun violence? According to one study, the number of deaths by gunshot in cattle towns during the year 1870-1885 were as follows:

Abilene - 7
Ellsworth - 6
Wichita - 4
Dodge City - 15
Caldwell - 13 [42]

In all of these five busy cattle towns, there were a total of forty-five homicides spread over fifteen years or a total of only three homicides per year. The population of the cattle towns was small, even so, the total number of deaths by shooting was low, not what you would expect from the gun violence pictured in Western novels, films, and television.[43]

---

42 Robert R. Dykstra, *The Cattle Towns* (Lincoln, NE: The University of Nebraska Press, 1983), 144.

43 Eric Hobsbawn, "The Myth of the Cowboy" (*The Guardian*, March 20, 2013). www.theguardian.com > profile > eric_ho…

Colt and Winchester, the gun manufacturers, boldly advertised their firearms. Winchester used the slogan "The Gun That Won the West" for its successful rifle. They made sure the word got out that, besides the revolver, law enforcement officers found it necessary to carry their rifles. Colt had the single-action army revolver and advertised it as the "Peacemaker." It was popular with cowboys, lawmen, and outlaws. But even with the increase in sales, which added to the possession of guns in the Old West, it was nowhere near, on a per capita basis in the United States today. In 2018, the Small Arms Survey estimated there were approximately 393 million firearms in the US, and with a population of about 326 million, that means 120.5 firearms for every one hundred US civilians. There were more firearms in the US than people.[44] We do not know the number of guns in the cattle towns, but it probably was not as great as what we have in the US today. The Wild West was not as violent as portrayed by the media.

FEELINGS, PERCEPTIONS, AND BEHAVIOR

Myth: The life of the cowboys was exciting and glamorous

The working conditions in the Wild West colored what the cowboys thought about themselves, their hopes and dreams, and their surroundings. Here, a distinction has to be made between the labor done at or near the ranch house and the work done on the open range. The work on the ranch was on foot, not horseback. Cowboys performed tasks such as cutting and storing hay, repairing fences, and tending and feeding the animals, jobs found on a typical farm. It was mundane and unexciting. However, at the ranch house, there were amenities, whereas on the open range, there was nothing. Most of the work on the range was done on horseback. It was rough and strenuous, and although there was a bit of excitement, it was not glamorous. Two types of open-range work involved enormous amount of time, stress, and effort—the roundup and the long cattle drive or cattle drove.[45]

During the rapid expansion of the Old West, there was a proliferation of longhorns in the territory now known as Texas. All that was needed for cattle to breed was grass and water. Texas provided

---

44 Aaron Karp, "Estimating Global Civilian-held Firearms Numbers," Small Arms Survey Briefing Paper, June 2018. www.smallarmssurvey.org > files.

45 Drove means a group of cattle moving in a body. Drive and drove have the same meaning and are used interchangeably as in trail drive and trail drove.

the ideal setting with its mild climate and vast grassland with available water. Fencing was rare in those days, and with cattle capable of drifting 150 miles, ranchers found it impossible to keep them on their property. Periodically, it was necessary to collect these strayed cattle, and these efforts in the 1840s and 1850s were known as "cow-hunts." Once the cattle were collected, the next step was to sort them, retain your own, and deliver others to their rightful owners. However, some of the cattle were unmarked so it was impossible to determine their ownership. Consequently, a system was set up, and ranches began to develop their symbol of ownership, called a "brand."

After the Civil War, in the late 1860s, different ranches came together twice a year in the spring and fall to collect the strayed cattle. This procedure was called the "roundup." Besides finding, sorting, and returning cattle to their owners, collective steps were taken to brand all cattle to ensure rightful ownership. In the spring roundup, the livestock was separated by ownership, new calves were branded, and cattle destined for the market were shipped out. In the fall roundup, strayed cattle were again returned to their owners and new calves that had been born since the spring roundup and those that were missed were branded.

Branding during roundup

Branding is an unpleasant task. The calf has to be roped, dragged to the branding fire, and the hot iron applied to the calf's flank. The animal yelps and there is a puff of white smoke with the smell of burning hair and flesh. Then, a second cowboy uses a pocket knife and places an ownership mark on the calf's ear. Furthermore, if it is a male calf, the cowboy would cut off the testicles. Creosote dip is then applied on the cut to keep flies away. At this point, branding is completed, and the calf scampers off, looking for its mother.

No two brands could be alike, so with each ranch having its distinct brand, quarrels over ownership of wandering cattle were mitigated or prevented. Moreover, it eliminated the inviting opportunity for thieves to seek unmarked cattle. Steer theft was a persistent problem. Cattle ranchers cooperated and followed the industry-wide practice of branding, but Samuel A. Maverick, a rancher in south Texas, did not. Due to a financial arrangement, he owned four hundred cattle, but Maverick had no interest in them and left his herd unbranded and neglected. Residents of the region complained about these wandering cattle and referred to them as "one of Maverick's." After many complaints, Maverick sold his cattle and brand to another rancher. The new owner made a strenuous effort, gathered the strayed cattle, and used the brand "Maverick" on his cattle. People of the area began to refer to all unbranded cattle as "Maverick."[46] The word "maverick" has been adopted into the English language and means an independent person who does not go along with a group.

Depending on the number of cattle and calves, roundup could take up to a week. It was done on the open range, and cowboys ate and slept in the fields. Charles Goodnight, the first cattle rancher to settle in south Texas, developed an oxen-drawn mess wagon or "chuck wagon" to feed the cowboys. It was a wagon converted with built-in shelves, drawers, and a work table. Cookware, including a Dutch oven, was carried in the chuck wagon, and medical supplies and bed rolls were added. The chuck wagon became integral to the cowboy image and synonymous with outdoor eating. Today, events are held featuring Western music with outdoor barbecue dining, which is reminiscent of eating in the old chuck wagon style.

---

46 Dary, *Cowboy*, 138-39.

Chuckwagon

Before the Civil War, there was a growing demand for beef in the eastern US. After the war, with the settlement of a large number of people in the territory far west of the Mississippi, and with the expansion of the railroad, there was now the means to supply this demand. And the supply was there; it is estimated there were about 3.5 million to 4.75 million cattle in Texas. This created an urgent need to move cattle from the ranches to the nearest railheads so they could be transported to the slaughterhouses in the big cities. It was a lucrative business with rising prices for each head of cattle. Cattle worth three to four dollars a head would be thirty to forty dollars in Kansas City and St. Louis and as much as sixty dollars in Chicago.[47]

A massive movement of cattle began in the 1850s and lasted until the 1890s. Most of the work was done from 1870 to 1885. This cattle movement caught the interest of many Americans. Writers and the reading public romanticized the cattle drive, and an iconic image of the cowboy and its culture was created. *The Log of a Cowboy: A Narrative of the Old Trail Days* (1903) by Andy Adams describes a fictional cattle drive from Texas to Montana in 1882 and accurately describes the cowboy life on the trail. Adams was a cowboy, so the book is based on his experience. Unlike the other writers, he did not romanticize the cattle drive. A more famous novel about a cattle drive is Larry McMurtry's *Lonesome Dove* (1985), but it is more recent; there is a gap of eight decades between the two books. McMurtry was an

---

47 Frantz, *American Cowboy*, 27.

outsider, and he was critical of the trail drive, and like Adams, he found it unglamorous. Nonetheless, even though the trail drive work was found to be dreadful, it could be argued that the cowboy would never have become an American folk hero had it not been for the cattle drives and the trails over which they took place. The cattle drives have been a rich source of the cowboy image, and without them, there would not be much of a cowboy myth.

In about forty years, approximately twenty-seven million cattle were driven from southern Texas to railheads in Kansas, then shipped to St. Louis on the way to Chicago and other eastern destinations. Cattle could only be moved at a certain rate, and it was determined that the optimal rate of movement was fifteen miles per day. Longhorns could move up to twenty-five miles per day by shortening their grazing and resting periods, but by doing this, the cattle dropped considerable weight. Since steers were sold by weight, the owners would lose large amounts of money; it was not economical. Therefore, the rate of fifteen miles per day was maintained, a balance between the speed and the weight of cattle. At this pace, it meant it would take two or three months for most cattle drives to travel from the home ranch to a railhead. The most famous cattle drive route, the Chisholm Trail, extended from the Rio Grande on the Mexican border to Abilene in Kansas, a distance of one thousand miles. It would take sixty-nine days to complete at fifteen miles per day. However, allowance for delays had to be considered because wind and rain could cause floods, dust storms, and other unpredictable hazards. Hence, it usually took ninety days.

Contemporary drawings showed the length of the stretched-out trail drive. Standing on a small hill, you could not see the end of the column of cattle, for it extended into the horizon. For those familiar with the work of the cowboy, it was an imposing sight, but for the uninitiated, it was frightening. A typical trail drive had around three thousand cattle and was managed by about a dozen cowboys called drovers. Therefore, there was one drover per 250-300 cattle. The crew of drovers consisted of the following:

- trail boss - usually rode ahead

- chuck wagon driver- positioned at the front

- horse wrangler - with the *remuda* (extra horses used to remount)

- point riders - two or more drovers to lead the cattle
- swing riders - two or more drovers to keep the herd in line
- flank riders - two or more drovers further back of the column
- drag riders - four or more drovers at the back to prevent stragglers[48]

The trail boss led the cattle drive and was responsible for delivering the herd to the railhead destination. He was at the front but could wander the length of the column to check and talk with the cowboys. Early in the morning, he scouted the route and returned before the crew was awake. The chuck wagon driver also got up early, at three o'clock in the morning, to prepare breakfast. During the day, at a scheduled time, he moved ahead to the next resting site and prepared for the team's arrival. Besides his primary role as a cook, he served as a first aid attendant because the wagon carried medical supplies. In addition, he was the storekeeper in charge of blankets and other riding equipment. For carrying out his diverse duties, he was the second-highest-paid drover, right below the trail boss. Since the cattle had to be watched day and night, the cowboys worked in shifts. When the shift ended, it was time to rest his horse. With the next shift, the rider had to remount a reserve horse, and in this task, he had the help of the wrangler. Sometimes, the reserve horse was feisty and difficult to handle, requiring some adjustment. The horse wrangler took care of the *remuda,* the riding stock, which could total sixty-five to one hundred horses. Fresh horses were necessary so the riders could prevent the cattle from wandering and protect the herd from predators and thieves. Point riders were experienced cowboys at the front. In contrast, drovers at the back were young and inexperienced cowboys. The tail end of the trail drive was an uncomfortable place. Dust kicked up by the cattle was horrendous; they would be coated with fine particles of dirt. For their work, inexperienced cowboys were paid $25 to $30, veteran cowboys $40, and the trail boss $125 per month.[49]

Cattle driving has existed since the beginning of the cattle industry. In the early cattle drives, the distances were shorter, and there were fewer cattle. The first long-distance drive took several months between 1853 and 1854. It was the longest cattle drive ever made in the US. Organized by Thomas Candy Ponting and his partner, Washington Malone, they bought seven hundred longhorns, started from northeast

48 Dary, *Cowboy*, 190-91.
49 Frantz, *American Cowboy,* 37-39.

Texas, and went northward to Illinois, crossing the Mississippi River at St. Louis by boat with their cattle. They wintered in Illinois and sold most of the cattle, keeping 150. Then, they covered the last leg from Muncie, Indiana to New York City by train. There were 130 cattle left to be sold. It must have been shocking to see longhorns roaming the streets of New York City. The full story of the Ponting drove was published in the *New York Daily Tribune* on July 4, 1854.[50] Ponting was not happy about all the publicity. He insisted the buyers not be informed that the cattle were from Texas, for it would lower the cattle price. Although it was a commercial success for Ponting and his supporters, and it did arouse curiosity, it did not, however, have an economic impact nationally. Cattle drives were already planned, organized, or underway in Texas. Still, it was the beginning of cattle drive stories that highlighted the cowboys' individualistic freedom and indomitable spirit.

The earliest and easternmost route was the Shawnee Trail (also known as Sedalia Trail), which started near San Antonio, passed through Waco and Dallas, through Indian Territory (Oklahoma), and ended at the railhead in Sedalia, Missouri. The most famous trail drive was the Chisholm Trail, which began from south Texas near the Mexican border and went through Ft. Worth, Texas, across the Red River into Oklahoma, and ended at the Kansas railheads at Abilene and Ellsworth. Jesse Chisholm started the trail when he established a wagon road around 1864, and by 1869, the trail became known as the Chisholm Trail. But it took Joseph G. McCoy, an astute businessman, to recognize that the endpoint was more important than the starting point. If the stockyards were built, the cattle would come. McCoy built shipping yards in Abilene, and they became a major center for cattle shipping, handling over thirty-six thousand cattle in the first year of operation. Abilene became the first nationally known cow town. The Chisholm Trail itself was relatively safe, and contrary to the belief that Native Americans would attack and steal cattle, there were few incidents. The Native Americans allowed the trail drive to go through their territory for a toll charge of ten cents a head.[51]

---

50 Dary, *Cowboy,* 14.
51 For a detailed account of *the Chisholm Trail, see* Sam P. Ridings, *The Chisholm Trail: A History of the World's Greatest Cattle Trail* (New York: Skyhorse Publishing, 2015). See also Frantz, *American Cowboy,* 31.

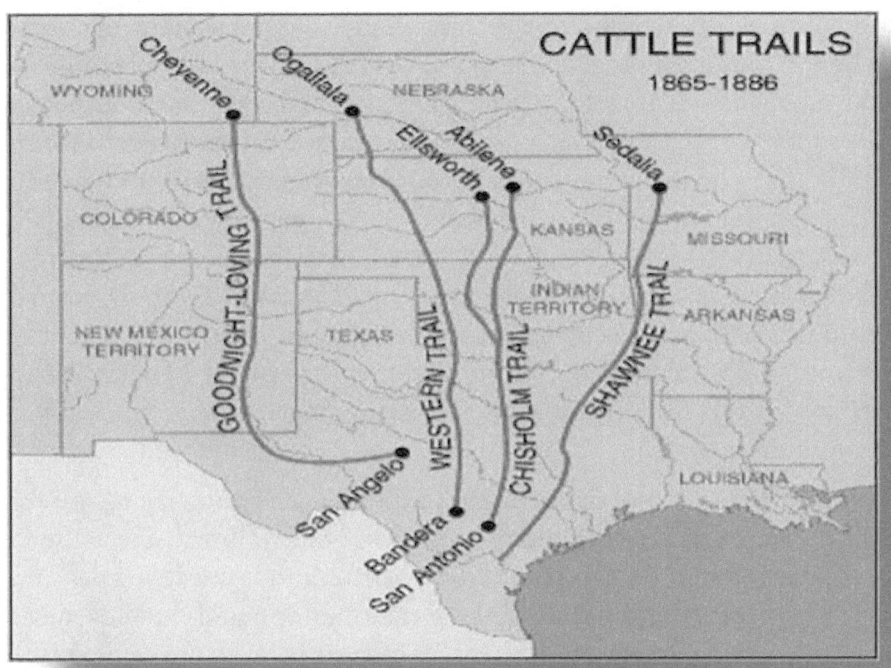

Map of cattle trail drives

By 1871, after only four years, the Chisholm Trail lost its importance due to the expansion of the railroad. New settlements opened west of Abilene, resulting in Dodge City, Kansas, becoming a more convenient railhead. A new trail was opened and ran west and roughly parallel to the Chisholm Trail. It was known as the Great Western Cattle Trail and started from Brownsville near the Mexican border and ended at the railhead in Ogallala, Nebraska. But its principal terminal was Dodge City, which became the hub of the cattle business. It took the cattle drive almost one hundred days to travel from south Texas to Dodge City. Railroad expansion continued westward and another railhead was opened in 1873 in Wichita, Kansas. In its first year as a railhead, Wichita received sixty-six thousand cattle and, the following year, seventy thousand heads of cattle.

Another cattle trail of renown was the Goodnight-Loving Trail, which was discussed in the first section of this chapter. These four trails, the Shawnee, Chisholm, Great Western, and Goodnight-Loving, were considered the "big four." There were others, some extending up to Montana, but they did not involve massive movement of cattle. Maps of the trails used by the cattle droves are perplexing because of the many lines denoting the principal routes and their many offshoots. A journalist, Harry Chrisman, wrote about several of the lesser-known trails that emanated north of Texas. Native Americans and wagon trains of the settlers first used them. Then, men involved in buffalo hunting utilized the paths, but once the buffalo herds were decimated, they shifted to the range cattle industry. Thousand of hoofs created deep ruts, and trails were fifty yards to two miles wide and were clearly defined.[52] The descriptions of life on the minor routes were similar to those on the well-known paths—the cattle drives were tough and not glamorous.

By 1885, the trail drives began to decline. The principal reason for the decrease was the continuing expansion of the railroad. The railroad companies began to transport herds of cattle, and it was less expensive. Moreover, many communities along the trails opposed the movement of cattle through their cities, towns, and farms because of "Texas fever," a disease spread by ticks that fell off the cattle. The longhorns were immune to the ticks, but cows and other farm animals in Arkansas, Missouri, Kansas, and Nebraska were not. Once contracted, the disease was often fatal. State legislatures passed quarantine laws restricting passage, and undoubtedly these restrictions were a factor in the eventual ending of the cattle-trailing industry. In addition, the cattle were doing damage by plodding through farms. Farmers in these states mounted vigorous protests, blocked the route, and even killed cattle. Other factors, such as men's misuse of natural resources and severe weather conditions, took their toll, Overgrazing, drought, and the winter of 1886-1887 wiped out many cattle businesses in the upper Great Plains and Montana. And finally, barbed wire greatly restricted the use of the open range. Joseph F. Glidden improved the wire fence by placing barbs along a wire and then twisting another wire around it to keep the barbs in place. He has been credited as the inventor of the modern barbed wire. The wire was effective and injured riders and animals that brushed against it. Most importantly, it changed the cattle business by preventing cattle from roaming freely. Barbed wire fencing blocked off large sections of land, and without open grazing range, cattle could no

---

52 Harry E. Chrisman, *Lost Trails of the Cimarron*. 2nd ed. (Norman, OK: University of Oklahoma Press, 1964), 57-61.

longer be moved on the trail; consequently, the cattle drive came to an abrupt end. A simple, unsophisticated technology helped bring down a thriving industry.

The myth examined in this section stated that the life of the cowboys was exciting and glamorous. What did the cowboys, personally think about their experience on the trail drive? We can refer back to the cowboy, Andy Adams, who worked on the cattle drive. He presented a picture of how brutal conditions were in his novel. Most of the cowboys did not record their experiences, but there are some notes, letters, diaries, and recorded interviews. The songs they sang at campfires during the cattle drives reflected the pathos, dreariness, and bitterness of the cowboy's life:

"The Kansas Line"

Come all you jolly cowmen, don't you want to go
Way up on the Kansas line?
Where you whoop up the cattle from morning till night
All out in the midnight rain.

The cowboy's life is a dreadful life,
He's driven through heat and cold;
I'm almost froze with the water on my clothes,
A-ridin' through heat and cold.

I've been where the lightnin', the lightnin' tangled in my eyes,
The cattle I could scarcely hold;
Think I heard my boss man say:
"I want all brave-hearted men who ain't afraid to die
To whoop up the cattle from morning till night,
Way up on the Kansas Line."

Speaking of your farms and your shanty charms,
Speaking of your silver and gold,—
Take a cowman's advice, go and marry you a true and lovely little wife,
Never to roam, always stay at home;
That's a cowman's, a cowman's advice,
Way up on the Kansas line.

Think I heard the noisy cook say,
"Wake up, boys, it's near the break of day,"—
Way up on the Kansas line,
And slowly we will rise with the sleepy feeling eyes,
Way up on the Kansas line.

The cowboy's life is a dreary, dreary life,
All out in the midnight rain;
I'm almost froze with the water on my clothes,
Way up on the Kansas line.[53]

---

53 Dary, 195-96. Quoted from John A. Lomax, *Cowboy Songs and Other Frontier Ballads* (New York: Sturgis & Walton Co., 1911), xix.

How perilous were the conditions on the trail drove? Cowboys had to ride through thick, thorny brushes, swift flooding rivers, blizzards, thunder, and dust storms. And there was always the relentless heat of the summer, the dangers of fires, or the bitter cold of the winter. In addition to the weather was the threat of stampedes—longhorns reacting to sudden noise, strong gusts of wind, animal attacks, or other disturbances. How the lead steer at the front reacted was critical. If it suddenly moved quickly in another direction, it could cause a stampede. River crossing with the herd was a complex problem—it required an assessment of the depth of the water, the speed of the current, and the steepness of the banks. It was probably the most difficult challenge faced by the drovers.

High on the list of factors affecting living conditions was the quality of the food. "Chuck" is the cowboy word for food. The cowboys were adequately fed, for the owners knew food was essential to maintain morale and productivity. But the food was unhealthy. Without refrigeration, it was impossible to have fresh fruits or vegetables. Their diet consisted of beef jerky (also known as salted meat), salted pork, mast-fed bacon, corn meal, rice, beans, sorghum molasses, dried fruits, coffee, and sourdough from which biscuits, bread, and flapjacks were made. While on the trail, they picked up supplemental foodstuffs, including boiled potatoes, brown gravy, light bread, and whatever killing they made of buffalo or deer.[54]

Since the herd had to be watched day and night, the working hours were long, even with shifts. Watching so many cattle was continually stressful, but there were also periods when boredom and loneliness set in. A constant complaint was lack of sleep. Sleeping on bedrolls on the ground without a tent was uncomfortable. The cowboys often went ninety days without bathing. Living conditions were rough and dirty. And they were inadequately compensated for this demanding work, earning thirty to forty dollars monthly. They were grossly underpaid and overworked. Most cowboys did not last long, averaging about seven years. The cowboy's life was neither glamorous nor exciting, and most were eager to leave the job.

---

54 Frantz, *American Cowboy*, 37.

Myth: Cowboys were virtuous with integrity and common sense

Generally speaking, Americans believed cowboys were practical, courageous, and fair-minded, but contrary to popular belief, many of the cowboys lacked these virtues and were immature. They were young, averaging about twenty-four, single, and tended to be uneducated drifters with little skills. Until 1885, cowboys had a negative image and were described in derogatory terms. Many were called cattle thieves. They were unjustly despised in American newspapers and pictured as wild, drunken ruffians because of their behavior in the cattle towns. However, the image of the undisciplined cowboy was rehabilitated by pulp magazines, novels, Wild West shows, and rodeos, which depicted them as heroic and brave figures with natural wisdom and virtues.[55]

The behavior of the cowboys could not be dismissed by the residents of the cattle towns. The young cowboys fell far short of being paragons of virtue and integrity. Their behavior was so atrocious the residents filed complaints. For the cowboys, the time-consuming and energy-draining trail drive physically and mentally exhausted them and brought out their worst. They were paid at the end of the trip, and with cash on hand, it was time to celebrate. After two or three months on the trail, they were ready for a good time. Their time was spent drinking, gambling, dancing, and frequenting the bordellos. Boisterousness ensued, and it did not take long for the cowboys to spend all their money.

The townsfolk resented the rowdy behavior of the cowboys but could not take any action since the town's economy depended on the cowboys. These communities arose at or near the railhead in anticipation of the cowboys' arrival with their cattle herd. Their sole purpose was to cater to the cattle industry, especially to the needs and wants of the cowboys. Three cattle towns became the major hubs—Abilene, Dodge City, and Wichita. Abilene, with a population of five hundred, had thirty-two saloons and many houses of prostitution. Dodge City had fourteen saloons, two dance halls, and several bordellos. Wichita had about twenty-eight saloons and a good share of prostitution houses. Without the cowboys' spending, the cattle towns' businesses would suffer, and the communities would find it difficult to survive.

---

55 Paul H. Carlson, "Myth and the Modern Cowboy," in *The Cowboy Way: An Exploration of History and Culture,* ed. Paul H. Carlson (Lubbock, TX: Texas Tech University Press, 2006), chap. 1.

Quarrels and fistfights occurred, but not as frequently as depicted in movies, and surprisingly, there were few deaths. There were fewer deaths from violence per capita in the cattle towns than in a modern American city or town. Even crimes like bank robberies were rare. Hollywood gave a different impression with the multitude of fight scenes and bank robberies in a typical Western movie. In reality, there was usually only one bank in town, and it was centrally located, making robberies improbable. Besides, the bank did not have much cash. Residents preferred to hold on to their cash and hide it. One man decided to hide his money under a fence post. He dug out the post, buried the money in the hole, and replaced the post. A few months later, he needed the cash but could not remember under which post he buried it. He completely tore up his fencing before he found the money.[56] Despite the carousing behavior of the cowboys, crime in the cattle town was not as common as many Americans believed.

Easterners who visited the cattle towns found them very different from their cities and towns. They were fascinated by cattle town cowboys with their strange large hats, boots with spurs and holsters with six-shooters. On the surface, it looked romantic, colorful and exciting. They wrote back to their readers, and to make it more interesting, they exaggerated what they had observed. Thus, the mythical cowboy and its culture were created. But in the real world, the cowboys, especially the young, inexperienced ones, were engaging in vices and some became victims of the vices. Although precise figures are lacking, there is a correlation between the increasing number of bordellos and the rise in venereal diseases. A US cavalry fort in the region reported more venereal diseases among its recruits. It was common in the Old West, and many cowboys were ravaged by diseases.

In summary, the myths covered in this chapter varied widely—some have kernels of truth and some validity, while others are completely divorced from reality. The American cowboy is a hybrid development heavily indebted to the Mexican vaqueros' culture, tradition, practices, and language. Cowboys are not an all-white group but are comprised of Mexican *vaqueros*, African Americans, and Native Americans. The horse remains an integral part of the cowboy image, but cowboys were

---

56 Dary, 167. Quoted from John Marvin Hunter, ed., *The Trail Drivers of Texas* (New York: Argosy-Antiquarian Press, 1963), 1:177.

not gunfighters or proficient with guns. Gunfights were not common, and duels were rare. The cowboys' life was not glamorous or exciting. Instead, it was boring, and the work was fraught with danger on the trail drive. The work conditions were terrible, with long hours and exposure to all kinds of weather. And finally, the cowboy was not a virtuous individual. He was young, immature, and open to vices. Considering the stress he was under, he tried to do his best but fell short and had regrets.

Ironically, the modernizing factors that brought about cowboys were the same factors that led to its demise. The expansion of the railroad westward created towns and cities as Americans moved into the plains. Moving into the open territory to escape the stresses of urban life with its social constraints led to the possession of the open range and the closure of the frontier. The increased population resulted in a huge demand for beef, thus developing the need for cattle drives. However, as the railroads continued to expand, it became possible to move cattle by rail, which was faster and cheaper. As a result, the cattle droves came to an end, and so did the cowboys. The wonders of nature, the vast, wide-open land, were no more. In the clash between nature and civilization, civilization won. The cowboy who had an affinity for nature and the wide-open space saw his way of life disappear, and soon he disappeared.

The mythical cowboy never physically existed. Yet it came to represent a relatively small group of real cowboys, approximately thirty thousand, who were on the scene for only three decades. Although they played a role in the expansion of the West, they had no political impact, and their social and economic influences were minimal. But the mythical cowboy gave Americans a "good" feeling. Today, that feeling has been diminished, and the model is problematic. Some would say it is irrelevant to contemporary society. Still, for many Americans and throughout the world, the purported "cowboy spirit" continues to endure.

The American cowboy myth lives on, but it is not the tangible but the intangible qualities that persist. Most American when they hear the word "cowboy" do not think in negative terms, but sees the cowboys as pioneers, exhibiting an individualistic spirit, a willingness to work, and an indomitable spirit to venture into new areas. In the past, it was the desire to step into the vast open territory with an acceptance and appreciation of the natural surroundings and the forces of nature. This attitude or frame of mind continues. For example, Americans today consider the space program a challenge to explore new frontiers with the same "cowboy spirit." The cowboy outlook continues.

PART II

SAMURAI

Chapter Four

Feudal Samurai

"Samurai" is a word that has been adopted by the English language and is known throughout the world. It is derived from the verb *saburau* (to serve), and in early Japanese history, it was used in reference to an individual who attends or performs services for another person of superior rank or status. One of the services rendered was defense or protection, executed by an elite military unit. The verb *saburau* was employed to describe the performance of security functions by a defense unit which became known as the samurai. At first, another word, "*bushi*" (military gentry) was used for this military group. Japanese still use "*bushi*" today, but it is not as popular, and few Americans are familiar with the word, although they may have heard of Bushido (warrior code). The term "*bushi*" first appeared in the late tenth-century chronological history of the Heian period (791-1185). The term "samurai" did not appear until later when it was first used in conjunction with nonmilitary service rendered by the retainer to his lord in the imperial court. It was a subordinate relationship with mutual obligations, a departure from relationships based on familial and kinship ties. By the twelfth century, the services rendered became exclusively military. "Samurai" became the designation for the direct vassals of the feudal lords, and they became the elite warrior class. Although the words *bushi* and samurai are not the same etymologically, they are used interchangeably and have the same meaning—the military elite. Nevertheless, understanding how the terms were first used helps explain the origin of the samurai.

For nine centuries, the samurai slowly evolved and established itself in Japanese society and came to rule the country. In contrast, historical cowboys spanned for only about forty years. Since the history of the samurai is long and extensive, a slightly different format is used in this chapter and the succeeding chapter.

ORIGIN AND DEVELOPMENT

A look at maps of early premodern Japan, roughly from the tenth to the seventeenth centuries, shows a proliferation of provinces or domains covering the four main islands of Japan, an area the size of California. With so many domains and the lack of a viable central government, the possibility of local protests, riots, and frictions between provinces arising was a constant and troubling concern. Means to stem and control local and regional disturbances were unavailable. Policing and a defense organization were needed to hinder and deter potential threats.

T'ang China had developed a centralized government with ministries to handle policing and defensive needs. The Japanese tried to copy the Chinese model but found the geographical context to be so different it was impossible to implement the Chinese example. The central government in Kyoto tried to conscript a defensive force, but it did not work and was abandoned. Then, the emperor and his imperial household appointed courtiers as provincial governors to administer and control the outlying provinces. However, the courtiers did not want to go into the provinces and instead delegated local officials to act in their stead. Political power was gradually transferred to the local elites, which happened to be the military elites, the samurai.

At first, the Japanese created local defense units, the *bushidan* or warrior bands. They were family or kinship-based organizations, what we would call civilian, family-based militia. When an emergency arose, and they were called up, they had to leave their work. In areas with a shortage of people, these interruptions severely disrupted the economy. When the fighting ended, the *bushidan* members would return to work, but the damage was done. Despite its limitations, the *bushidan* was the first step, and its members were the forerunners of the samurai.

By the eleventh century, the defense organizations had developed into more permanent military units. Within each unit, close master-servant relationships were formed. Why did such a relationship form? Protection of land holdings and livelihood was the principal reason. The servant had no means to protect himself; he had to rely on his lord. Already, a bond of loyalty had been formed from the battlefield experiences. Similar to a contractual agreement between the servant or vassal and the owner or lord, it differs from the earlier forms of relationship based on family or common ancestry. No longer is it based on family ties. It is now a formal relationship with undying loyalty. It is the beginning of the samurai.

Scholars have described the time from the Kamakura period (1185-1333) to the Tokugawa period (1603-1868) as Japan's feudal period. The concept of feudalism is most often applied to Western Europe of the medieval period, the so-called Middle Ages. During the same period in world history, feudal practices emerged in Japan but differed from those in Europe. Still, there are similarities, such as the emergence of an armored horse-riding military class—knights in Europe and samurai in Japan, and the knight's chivalric code of honor and the samurai's Bushido. Applying the concept of feudalism to Japan has limitations, but even so, the idea is helpful in understanding what took place during this period of history.

Initially, a series of disturbances occurred among clans in the Kanto region (eastern Honshu). Fighting continued and expanded into other area and by the twelfth century, a few warrior armies had become the dominant force throughout the country. A major reason for the rise of the samurai class was the weakness of the courtier-controlled government in Kyoto. The Imperial Court failed to maintain adequate administration of the provinces. The provincial samurai became autonomous centers of power. Emperors and their supporters twice resisted and fought battles with the local samurai units. The first imperial attempt was quickly stopped, and the second attempt, although initially successful, was eventually defeated.

After periodic armed clashes between competing samurai groups, two clans emerged dominant. Taira (also known as Heike) in western Japan was led by Taira no Kiyomori (1118-1181). He was appointed prime minister, the highest position held by a samurai in the central government. The other clan was Minamoto in eastern Japan. Samurai comprised the bulk of these warrior armies. They pledged their loyalty to their lord and, when appropriate, were rewarded for their loyal service with grants of land. At first, the Taira clan was victorious, but in a series of crucial battles in the Genpei War (1180-1185), the Taira was crushed. From these battles rose one of the greatest and most popular Japanese heroes, Minamoto no Yoshitsune (1159-1189). He helped his half-brother Yoritomo (1147-1199) secure power. Soon after, Yoritomo established the Kamakura bakufu, the first military government to rule Japan.

Minamoto no Yoshitsune

Minamoto no Yoritomo

Even though Yoritomo was the supreme ruler, he was suspicious of Yoshitsune and took action to limit his influence. Yoshitsune fought back but had to flee and sought protection in the residence of one of his allies. The son of the ally betrayed Yoshitsune, and Yoshitsune and his retainers found themselves surrounded and were quickly subdued. Yoshitsune was forced to commit *seppuku* (*harakiri* or disembowelment), and his decapitated head was sent to Yoritomo as proof of his death.[57]

The stories did not end. Legends claimed Yoshitsune did not commit *seppuku* but escaped to Hokkaido or mainland Asia. He appears in the literary classic *Heike Monogatari* (*The Tale of the Heike*) and the writings of the fourteenth century, such as *Gikeiki* (*Chronicle of Yoshitsune*). These literary works about Yoshitsune are often legends and not based on historical facts. Yoshitsune is the subject of a Noh play and is featured in the kabuki play *Kanjincho*. His adulation continued into modern times. Akira Kurosawa, the renowned film director,

---

57 George Bailey Sansom, *A History of Japan to 1334* (Stanford: Stanford University Press, 1958), 258-60, 291. Hiroaki Sato, *Legends of the Samurai* (New York: Overlook Duckworth, 1995), 110-56. Sato translated sections from the *Azuma Kagami* ("Mirror of the East"), a chronicle of the Kamakura period, and contributed valuable commentaries.

adapted *Kanjincho* into the movie *The Men Who Tread on the Tiger's Tail* (1945). While these works have some historical truths, writers had taken the liberty of embellishing Yoshitsune's life. But this is the process by which national heroes are created. Yoshitsune became the exemplar samurai—the mythical samurai. He is one of Japan's tragic heroes. After achieving spectacular victories in battles at the height of his career, he was opposed by his half-brother, betrayed, and forced to commit suicide. Yoshitsune died at the young age of thirty. Ivan Morris, a noted translator and Japan scholar, cites Yoshitsune as a prime example of a failed hero. He could not reach his goal of serving in the military government for all of Japan. Nevertheless, the Japanese people respect and admire an individual who fights bravely, is resolute in carrying out his task, and is absolutely dedicated and loyal.[58]

The Kamakura *bakufu,* formed by Yoritomo, began the long line of military rule in Japan. "*Bakufu*" means military field headquarters and is sometimes translated as "tent government." Yoritomo's *bakufu* became the de facto ruler of Japan. He exercised complete political power, and the emperor in Kyoto was relegated to a symbolic status, a figurehead. Yoritomo assumed the title of shogun (military commander) in 1192; for the most part, it was a hereditary position. The government was called the shogunate.

The Kamakura shogunate lasted for 148 years. There were endless intrigues, factional conflicts, assassinations, and a war between the emperor and the shogunate. The Fujiwara clan replaced the Minamoto clan, and in turn, the Fujiwara was replaced by the Hojo clan. The Fujiwara and the Hojo exercised political power as regents to the shogun. In 1333, Emperor Go-Daigo raised a samurai army against the shogunate. At this juncture, a samurai leader appeared who would become one of Japan's most illustrious heroes; he was the noted military strategist Kusunoki Masashige (1294-1336). He was one of the first to respond to the emperor's summon and led the fight to overthrow the shogunate and restore power to the emperor. In the initial battle, Kusunoki faced a superior shogunate army and eventually fled, and the emperor was captured. He continued the struggle and won a strategic battle against more significant shogun forces by cunningly employing guerrilla tactics. Kusunoki utilized the terrain to his advantage and

---

58 Ivan N. Morris, *The Nobility of Failure: Tragic Heroes in the History of Japan* (New York: Holt, Rinehart and Winston, 1945), 67.

engaged the enemy by ambushes and hit-and-run tactics, thereby minimizing the lack of a larger army. Deception was used such as placing dummy warriors as a decoy to lure the enemy into the open. These actions were highly successful, and Kusunoki emerged as a respected guerrilla tactician.

Meanwhile, the emperor managed to escape. Ashikaga Takauji (1305-1358), the commander of a large force, was dispatched to recapture the emperor, but Takauji turned against the shogunate and easily captured Kamakura, the shogunate's capital. He destroyed the Hojo family, which had controlled the shogunate, thus ending the Kamakura bakufu. This power play was typical of the political scene at that time when the thirst for power led leaders to take advantage of any opportunity.

Kusunoki Masashige's statue, Imperial Place grounds

Takauji convinced other military leaders that power should not be returned to the emperor. In 1335, Emperor Go-Daigo went against Takauji and had Kusunoki lead the imperial forces. Kusunoki defeated Takauji's army in January 1336, but a few months later, Takauji returned with a much larger force. Kusunoki realized he could not win against a vastly superior army and wanted to retreat to a more favorable terrain, but the emperor insisted that Kusunoki remain in place and attack Takauji. Despite knowing it would mean sure defeat, Kusunoki led the charge in the Battle of Minatogawa. He fought bravely, but was overwhelmed by the numerically larger foe. Rather than being captured, he committed *seppuku*.

Here, we have another tragic hero. Kusunoki Masashige is considered to be one of the most famous samurai warriors. Yet he was on the losing side, lost the battle, and committed suicide. Even so, he was a loyal, obedient warrior. It took two and a half centuries before Kusunoki became a widely recognized hero. Sato Hiroaki, poet, translator and journalist, describes Kusunoki as a "guerrilla of unflinching loyalty."[59] He knew the best way to fight was to retreat and use guerrilla tactics, but when ordered to fight, he obeyed even though the odds were against him. He was willing to follow orders, go all out, and fight for his cause. It reminds me of a slogan I often heard while undergoing officer training at Ft. Benning, Georgia: "Ours is not to reason why, ours is but to do and die."

The myth of Kusunoki was extolled by the Japanese armed forces in World War II. The kamikaze attacks during the Battle for Okinawa and Lieutenant General Kuribayashi Tadamichi's final Iwo Jima attack order are reminiscent of Kusunoki's tragic, heroic act. The Battle of Iwo Jima was the subject of two films, back-to-back, directed by Clint Eastwood, *Flags of Our Fathers* (2006) from the perspective of the American invaders and *Letters from Iwo Jima* (2006) from the viewpoint of the Japanese defenders. In the *Letters from Iwo Jima,* the role of General Kuribayashi was acted by Ken Watanabe. Most Japanese, including critics, agree that the portrayal of the general was sympathetic and accurate. Especially poignant was his confrontation with death and the final attack order. The film was widely acclaimed in Japan.

At the beginning of the Iwo Jima battle, Kuribayashi opted for a dug-in defensive strategy. He had learned that aggressive "banzai charges" were unsuccessful in Guadalcanal and Saipan. But at the end, reduced to a few men, he ordered the final charge and committed suicide. This action encompasses a concept known as *gyokusai* (shattered jewels), where there is no hope of surviving, and one is ordered to fight to the

---

59 Sato, *Legends,* 157.

death. Since surrender is not an option, it means total annihilation. *Gyokusai* resulted in group suicide, so perhaps a better translation of *gyokusai* would be "honorable death in combat." The Japanese military used this meaning and linked it with service to the emperor.[60] It could be applied to civilians and aesthetically defined as shattering oneself like a beautiful jewel to achieve a common objective. Death is seen as a permanent state of perfection and is preferred to the conflicting and transitory nature of life. It is not always a maniacal "banzai charge," as it is often alluded; mass suicide could have a philosophic basis.[61]

With the elimination of the imperial threat, Ashikaga Takauji had complete political control, and he appointed himself as shogun. In 1338, he started the second military government, the Ashikaga shogunate, in Kyoto's nearby town of Muromachi. The Ashikaga shogunate lasted for fifteen generations but was an unstable government. It allowed Go-Daigo to escape, and he established an imperial court at Yoshino (present-day Nara). This Southern Court existed parallel with the Northern Court in Kyoto, which had Komyo as emperor. Consequently, for almost two decades, Japan had two reigning emperors.

More serious was the inability of the Ashikaga shogunate to halt or control warring factions throughout the provinces and even within the shogunate itself. Civil wars and social upheavals continuously occurred. The Onin War (1467-1477) was most damaging, wherein feudal lords and provincial governors throughout Japan took sides and fought each other. Historians agree the Onin War was the start of the Sengoku (Warring States) period, which continued until the late sixteenth century.[62]

Over a century of continuous fighting occurred during the Sengoku period, considered to be one of the most violent times in Japanese history. In the mid-sixteenth century, there were over 150 active feudal lords (*daimyo*). They were specifically referred to as *sengoku daimyo*

---

60 Kuribayashi Tadamichi, *"Gyokusai soshikikan" no etegami* (Tokyo: Shogakkan, 2002). Hiroaki Sato, "Gyokusai or 'Shattering Like a Jewel:' Reflection on the Pacific War." *Asia-Pacific Journal.* Japan Focus. February 1, 2008, vol. 6, issue 2. apjjf.org > hiroaki-sato > article.

61 "Banzai" is a slogan used in weddings and other ceremonies and means hurray! It became a battle cry of the Japanese armed forces and is a shortened version of *"Tenno heika banzai"* ("long live the emperor").

62 Many samurai films take place in the Sengoku period. It is the background of several Akira Kurosawa's movies, including the *Throne of Blood* (1957) and *Ran* (1985). When asked why, Kurosawa said he loves the period for its actions and intrigues. Sengoku battles were vicious, but Kurosawa did not go overboard with the brutality. The films supported as well as demolished some of the myths about the samurai.

and displaced the military governors (*shugo daimyo*) appointed by the shogunate in the mid-fourteenth century. Alliances were made and broken between the *sengoku daimyo* as they fought among themselves for regional hegemony. There were constant upheavals as *sengoku daimyo* were replaced by new ones, and in this period, a peasant could be elevated to a samurai and advance in status or to a high position. An obvious example was Toyotomi Hideyoshi (1537-1598), a peasant who rose to samurai rank and later became one of the three famous "unifiers of Japan."

Adding stress to this period of upheaval was the arrival of Portuguese traders and Jesuit priests in the mid-sixteenth century. Their effect on the samurai was twofold—the introduction of firearms impacted the samurai's role and function, and Christianity changed their attitudes about foreign influence. How the foreigners affected the myths of the samurai is explored in detail in the next chapter.

There was an immediate need to consolidate power throughout Japan to end the constant fighting. The movement to unify Japan under one dominant ruler was initiated by Oda Nobunaga (1534-1582) and almost fulfilled by Toyotomi Hideyoshi. The consolidation was completed and systematized by Tokugawa Ieyasu (1543-1616). This unifying movement started during the 1570s and extended into the 1590s.

Three Unifiers of Japan

The Three Unifiers of Japan
L to r: Oda Nobunaga, Toyotomi Hideyoshi, and Tokugawa Ieyasu.

The three unifiers were samurai but differed in personalities and backgrounds. Nobunaga rose from *jito* (deputy) to top military commander. He was a strategist and an advocate of foreign weaponry. The unifying process started with his defeat of the Ashikaga forces and the shogunate's end in 1573. By the 1580s, he had control over most of Honshu. Nobunaga was brutal and showed no mercy towards his enemies. He did not believe in taking prisoners, and in the battle at Mount Hiei, thousands of Buddhist monks were slaughtered. His brutal use of power made many enemies. In the end, he was betrayed by one of his generals. Nobunaga was surrounded in a temple, and he and his son decided to take the honorable way out by committing *seppuku*. Although Nobunaga did not follow the prescribed Confucian values of the samurai, he is still respected for his military successes.

The second unifier, Toyotomi Hideyoshi, started as a low-ranking samurai in Nobunaga's organization but rose to be one of his generals. He avenged Nobunaga's death by defeating the killer's army and bringing back the general's corpse as evidence. Hideyoshi used his diplomatic and military skills to gain hegemony over the two recalcitrant domains in Kyushu. In 1590, he finally took control of the eastern part of Honshu, which meant he had overcome opposition in all of the major parts of Japan. Hideyoshi solidified his power not only through battles but also through policy moves. Provincial armies were always potential threats and had grown more extensive with the enlistment of peasants. One way to control this threat was to take away their weapons. Hideyoshi ordered a "sword hunt" that effectively confiscated weapons from the peasantry. It essentially limited the fighting class in Japan to the samurai class. Further restrictions were instituted through house laws, which governed the responsibilities and activities of *daimyo* and their samurai. Moreover, there was a social stratification of four classes: samurai, farmer, artisan, and merchant, wherein no movement was allowed from one class to another.

There were thousands of low-ranking provincial samurai who lived among the farmers and owned land. They were the *jizamurai* (samurai of the land) who spent most of their time working the farm. An edict was issued that detached the samurai from their land and forced them to move into the castle town and attach themselves to a *daimyo*. This policy by Hideyoshi was ostensibly to eliminate the possibility of these low-ranking samurai joining the peasants in protest movements. When the samurai moved into the castle town and came under a *daimyo*, the bond between the samurai and his lord was tightened, and the samurai became totally dependent and subservient to the lord, thus undermining any connection with the peasants. In addition, the national cadastral survey impacted the samurai. Under the survey, arable land was measured for productivity, and an annual tax was assessed based on yield. Productivity was used as a basis for organizing the domains, and the larger or wealthier domains went to the *daimyo* closest and most loyal to Hideyoshi. This distribution affected the samurai because his only income was now the stipend, and the amount of the stipend was largely dependent on the wealth of the domain.

Hideyoshi was erratic and brutal in handling foreigners and his relationship with other countries. He persecuted and executed Jesuits, Franciscans priests, and Japanese Christians. In 1596, he ordered the crucifixion of twenty-six Christians in Nagasaki. He also sent thousands of samurai on an expedition to Korea to conquer China, but it developed into a stalemate and ended in failure. With his death in 1598, the question of succession arose since the only successor was his five-year-old son.

The third and final unifier of Japan was Tokugawa Ieyasu, who brought all of Japan under a military government. Ieyasu was an ally of Nobunaga and after his death, he allied with Hideyoshi. He became the most powerful *daimyo* in the Kanto area in eastern Honshu. The succession issue after the death of Hideyoshi was settled in the showdown between the Toyotomi and Tokugawa factions, a battle between the western (Toyotomi) and eastern (Tokugawa) armies. The epic battle took place at Sekigahara on October 21, 1600. Tokugawa Ieyasu emerged victorious. He took on the title of shogun in 1603 and established the Tokugawa shogunate, the third and longest military government in Japanese history. He brought on a remarkable period of peace and stability that lasted over 250 years.

A system called *bakuhan* (military government and domain) was implemented. Ieyasu took over Hideyoshi's policies, modified and expanded them, and most importantly, effectively had the policies carried out and enforced. Japan was divided into domains, each producing at least ten thousand *koku* (1 *koku* = 5 bushels) of rice annually. Therefore, to be a *daimyo,* a minimum of ten thousand *koku* was required. Wealth was measured by *kokudaka* (productivity assessment), the annual yield expressed in units of *koku* of rice. *Koku* was a simpler and easier measurement of wealth than money. The traditional formula is problematic, but one *koku* of rice is supposed to support one person for a year.

There were three categories of *daimyo* that the Tokugawa government used to distribute the confiscated lands of the defeated enemies. First, a portion went to the *shinpan daimyo*, its house-related *daimyo,* that is, relatives of the shogun. Another portion went to the *fudai daimyo,* the generals allied with Ieyasu at Sekigahara, essentially vassals of Ieyasu. The final allotment went to the *tozama daimyo,* those who were not allied with the Tokugawa house but only became allies after Sekigahara. This last group was the largest, and their total land yielded more than ten million *koku* annually. The Maeda daimyo in Kaga had land producing one million *koku,* making it the richest domain in the country. The generous amount given to the *tozama* kept them satisfied. Even though it had to be divided among a larger group of *daimyo,* it was still a significant amount. It was a carrot-and-stick policy, keeping them in control by offering generous inducements.

Ieyasu followed the social policies of Hideyoshi, further strengthened them, and enforced the practices more vigorously. The recruitment of soldiers was a continual concern. The rank and file of the domain army was composed of foot soldiers (*ashigaru*), increasingly recruited from the peasantry. During the Sengoku period, the *ashigaru* became prominent as armies grew larger. They were joined by the *jizamurai* who, given the condition of perpetual warfare, were occasionally forced to suspend their farm work and serve in the army. These part-time soldiers and the ashigaru were poorly trained and lowly regarded. The distinction between samurai and peasant foot soldiers became wider in 1588 when Hideyoshi banned commoners from possessing weapons, to prevent the possibility of armed peasant rebellion. but it had wider repercussions, for it coincided with a check on the *jizamurai.* Already under Hideyoshi, many of these low-ranking samurai were forced into castle towns, losing their land and falling under a new lord, but under Ieyasu the process was systematized and rigidly enforced. Those who remained outside were stripped of their samurai status and became peasant farmers. The *jizamurai* that moved into castle towns were considered samurai and paid stipends as compensation. In smaller domains with limited resources, stipends were small, and the samurai faced serious financial problems. They had to find other sources of income but lacked skills and even ambition. Some had better opportunities and became bureaucrats, administrators, and even entrepreneurs, but the majority found it difficult to transition. For the samurai desperate for a loan, it was humiliating to go the merchants at the bottom of the social structure. The changing conditions of the samurai led to continual grief and stress.

Social stability was a great concern for the shogunate, and policies were instituted to keep the *daimyo* and his retainers in check. Personal conduct, travel, dress, and marriage were prescribed. Castles could not be added or expanded, and the *daimyo* was required to participate in *sankin-kotai* (alternate attendance), where they resided in Edo (present-day Tokyo) in alternate years. Being in Edo meant closer surveillance of the *daimyo,* his family, and his vassals.

The social order in the Tokugawa period was formal and rigid. Social status was inherited with little social mobility. At the top were the emperor and court nobles (*kuge*) who had prestige but little power; the actual rulers were the shogun and *daimyo*. There were about 250 *daimyo*. The number could change slightly because, for example, a *daimyo* could lose his position and domain for gross misconduct. Below the *daimyo* were about four hundred thousand samurai; they were ranked by different grades and degrees. In both the Kamakura and Ashikaga shogunates, the vassals were known as *gokenin*. When the Tokugawa gained ascendancy, the upper-ranking vassals of the Tokugawa house became *hatamoto* (bannermen), while the lower-level vassals remained *gokenin*. The *hatamoto* were like staff members of the *daimyo*. High-ranking *hatamoto* had the privilege of an audience with the shogun, but the *gokenin* did not. It was rare, but there were a few individuals who were able to move from one classification to another. With the absence of warfare, it became difficult for any social mobility. While the social policies governing personal behavior, dress, and ranking played a part in establishing the image of the samurai, the policy that had the most impact on the image was the restriction that only the samurai were permitted to wear *daisho* (two swords). The sword became a status symbol.

The attitude of Japanese leaders towards foreigners and their religion, culture, and products played a part in the projected image of the ideal samurai. At first, the leaders eagerly accepted Western innovations. Nobunaga quickly adopted and used foreign weapons. A few samurai became enamored with Western technology and took up "Dutch Learning" at Deshima, a man-made, fan-shaped island in Nagasaki Bay. It was the only place where the Tokugawa government allowed foreign contact, but it was limited to trade and the exchange of information. Initially, the area housed the Portuguese traders, but they were expelled in 1639, and two years later, Dutch merchants were brought in as replacements. In addition, there were a few Chinese traders stationed on the island.

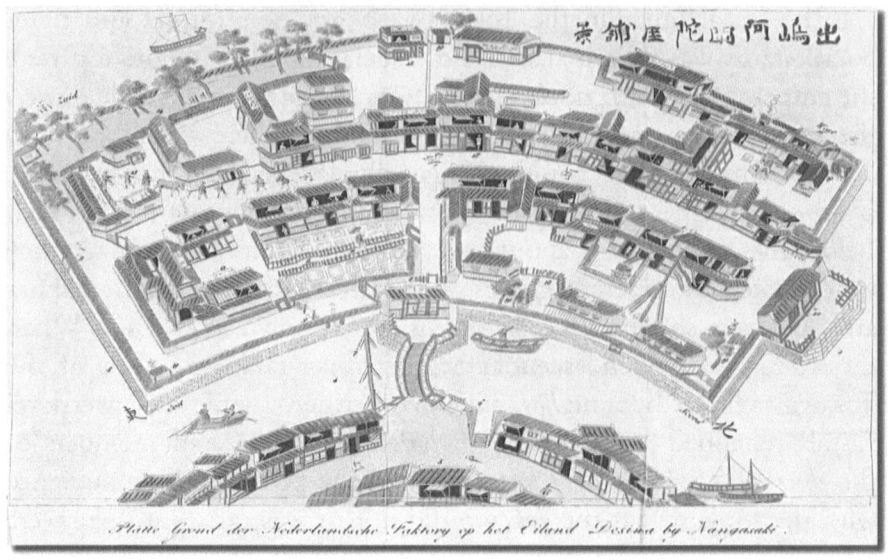

Deshima

Outside of Deshima, a small number of Japanese, such as Honda Toshiaki and Sato Nobuhiro, studied the Dutch language and read books on Western science and technology on their own. In their writings, they reflected on the challenges Japan faced in catching up with the West. The shogunate understood the importance of Western studies and had an agency created to translate Dutch books. However, the authorities became suspicious of European and American intrusions and that these activities might undermine the authority of the Japanese government. In 1614, the Tokugawa shogunate began to issue a series of edicts restricting contact with the West. The restrictions became more stringent with the Christian Expulsion Edict of 1633 and ended with the final policy of national seclusion in 1639; it was called *sakoku* (closed country). These edicts severely limited trade with foreign countries. Japanese were forbidden to travel abroad, priests and Christian missionaries were expelled, Christianity was banned, and Japanese Christians were persecuted and executed. Foreign religions were viewed as subversive threats to the government.

Meanwhile, samurai officials looked in the other direction and, increasingly intrigued by Confucian thoughts. There was a revival of Confucianism, but it took a new form, rejecting mysticism and adopting a rational and secular approach. It was known as Neo-Confucianism. The emphasis was on self-cultivation and harmonious social relationships. At this time, the Bushido (the way of the warrior), a moral and behavior code emphasizing loyalty, honor, honesty, respect, filial piety, and courage, was finally formalized and systematized. These virtues were clearly influenced by Confucian ideals. From the earliest days, samurai recognized and follow a set of values and ethics, but it was never formally written down. But now, in the seventeenth century, it was fully expressed. Although influenced by Shinto and Zen Buddhist thoughts, the Confucian values had the greatest impact.

In a pushback to Neo-Confucianism, a group of scholars instituted the school of *kogaku* (ancient studies) to advance and promote Japanese values and culture. It later became known as *kokugaku* (national study). *Kokugaku* looked back to ancient times when culture and society were free from foreign ideas, and Japan was "pure." It wanted to re-establish this "pure" Japanese culture. In a society where there was no warfare, hence no need for a warrior class, a rationale was needed to legitimize the role of the samurai. *Kokugaku* argued that the samurai were an essential part of the value system and culture of Japan and that they were required to uphold it. This was the rationale for the samurai class.

MYTHS AND REALITIES

In the close to one thousand years that the samurai had existed, there were striking changes in how Japanese and foreigners viewed the samurai. Images and myths were created, modified, and abandoned depending on circumstances, whether there were wars, absence of wars, or periods of agitation or complacency. First, there was the growing glorification of the samurai for their courage and loyalty displayed in frequent warfare. Heroes such as Yoshitsune and Kusunoki could emerge and become model samurai or, in a larger sense, mythical samurai. Second, there was the diminution of their role and the tarnishing of their image. The role of the samurai was lessened by the changing nature of warfare with larger armies and the introduction of new weapons and tactics. There were few sword fights, and when heroic actions took place, they were episodic and largely anonymous. Attempts were made to revive admiration for the samurai through the creation of a new ethos. Although somewhat successful, it could not stop the inexorable changes. Finally, it ended with the dissolution of the samurai class in the late nineteenth century. Therefore, significant changes occurred in the image of the samurai. Returning to basic myths surrounding the samurai is necessary to understand the devolution that transpired. What follows in this chapter are a few of the basic myths about the traditional samurai, the warrior of the premodern era. The modifications are discussed, and where pertinent, the basic myths are compared with the realities of samurai life and culture.

Myth: Loyalty is the highest virtue

Loyalty is a virtue or trait associated with the samurai from the earliest time. It was demanded of all warriors. Hence, it is not surprising that the samurai were characterized as loyal to their superior, the emperor or the feudal lord. This was the basis for the vassal-lord relationship. The historical chronicles cite many examples of samurai fealty, and the literature is replete with stories about the loyalty of retainers.

Perhaps the best exemplar of samurai allegiance is Kusunoki Masashige. As previously noted, Kusunoki was a successful guerrilla strategist. When faced with an overwhelming Ashikaga army, he thought it was prudent to retreat to a favorable terrain. The emperor ordered him to remain and take a stand against the enemy. This meant inevitable defeat, but Kusunoki complied. He showed extreme bravery, but more important was how he died and the circumstances under which it took place. If Kusunoki had followed his guerrilla strategy and successfully defeated the Ashikaga, he would have been admired for his bravery and military skills. But he would not have become a legendary heroic samurai. Kusunoki became the perfect hero, a model of ideal samurai behavior, because he showed that loyalty is the highest virtue and is unbounded and eternal. He was not only loyal to the emperor, but he was sincere in his loyalty to his profession. Kusunoki took the honorable way out by committing *seppuku* with his brother.

Kusunoki recognition as a national hero did not take place immediately. Nearly two and a half centuries after his death, he was finally given the honor. He could not be recognized as long as the Ashikaga remained in power. Ashikaga had to be considered the villain, and the delay was lengthy because the shogunate lasted 237 years. Finally, in 1563, with the Ashikaga falling apart, things began to change. Until now, Kusunoki was deemed a traitor and a rebel, but now he has been given a posthumous pardon. At the same time, the *Taiheiki* (*Record of Great Peace*), written in 1329 with descriptions of Kusunoki's exploits, became popular.[63] The *Taiheiki*, like most Japanese historical narratives, tends to exaggerate details, but for the most part, the text is considered accurate. It is from the *Taiheiki* that his often quoted: "He wished that he would be reborn seven times to fight for the emperor" is derived. This statement was later shortened to a slogan: "Would that I had seven lives to give to my country." In modern times, Japanese nationalists and pro-imperialists have used this slogan and followed the footsteps of Kusunoki.

For the Neo-Confucian writers of the Tokugawa period, Kusunoki provided a perfect example of the virtues of *ko* (filial piety) and *chu* (loyalty), which played a large part in the Bushido code. Filial piety is displayed in a well-known episode in *Taiheiki*, where Kusunoki writes a farewell poem to his eldest son, Masatsura, known as "*Sakurai no wake*," or "the parting at Sakurai," showing deep devotion between father and son. This scene has been depicted in literary and dramatic works, drawings and paintings, movies and television shows, and songs.[64]

When the Meiji government came to power in 1868, it was designated the Meiji Restoration because the emperor was restored. The Meiji government was particularly interested in one aspect of the Kusunoki myth—he fought for the emperor. No other samurai hero did this. Up to this point, samurai warriors fought for their *daimyo,* not the emperor. He was unique among Japanese heroic figures, exemplifying the Bushido virtues of loyalty, obedience, and sincerity. So, he was the ideal hero, combining the proper set of behavior with the correct purpose of defending the emperor.

Over five hundred years after his death, Kusunoki was given a high-ranking title in the imperial court, and an enormous statue was erected

---

63 Stephen Turnbull, *The Lone Samurai and the Martial Arts* (London: Arms and Armour, 1992), 149. Helen Craig McCullough, *The Taiheiki: A Chronicle of Medieval Japan* (Rutland, VT: Tuttle Publishing, 1979).

64 Turnbull, *The Lone Samurai*, 150. The writing of a farewell poem before going into battle was a tradition of the samurai from the early days and continued into modern times. Masatsura followed his father's example and wrote a farewell poem before he died in battle. He was twenty-two.

on the imperial palace ground facing Nijubashi (Double Bridge), leading to the main gate of the Imperial Palace. It is an impressive bronze sculpture with Kusunoki on a spirited horse in full armor, ready for combat.

Adulation of Kusunoki reached its peak in the 1930s, a period of extreme nationalism. Textbooks extolled his heroic deeds, and every student came to know Kusunoki. During the Pacific War, the Kusunoki stories inspired kamikaze pilots as they engaged in suicide attacks. The famous saying of Kusunoki: "The triumph of truth over wrong and the triumph of heaven over all," was inscribed in abbreviated form on the side of the one-man suicide bombers.[65]

In the aftermath of defeat in World War II, anything having to do with the military came under attack. The myth of Kusunoki was proscribed. The American Occupation censored stories about him from textbooks and banned literary works and stage plays that glorified him. Soon, the myth of Kusunoki faded from the memories of the Japanese.

Kusunoki was one heroic individual, but on a larger scale, the story of the Forty-Seven Ronin had a tremendous effect on the Japanese. It is a true story that extols the virtue of loyalty in the samurai class. The story began in 1701 in the shogun's castle in Edo. Asano Naganori, the *daimyo* of Ako, was in charge of a reception for the envoys from the Imperial Court in Kyoto, and the *daimyo* Kira Yoshinaka was instructing Asano on the ceremonies. There was disagreement between the two. Some say Kira resented Asano's defiance and decided to be boorish and abuse him. At the reception, Asano suddenly drew his short sword and attacked Kira, injuring him slightly. The reason for the attack is not known. Drawing a sword is forbidden under strict house rules, and Asano was ordered to commit *seppuku*. Kira did not receive any punishment. The shogunate confiscated Asano's lands, and the samurai who served him were dismissed, making them *ronin* (masterless samurai).

For the next fourteen months, the forty-seven or forty-six *ronin*, led by Oishi Kuranosuke Yoshio, a high-ranking samurai under Asano, prepared their revenge.[66] Oishi and the *ronin* changed their lifestyle

---

65 Turnbull, 150.

66 The figure of forty-six is used sometimes because some critics dismiss the membership of one member for various reasons. Oishi is the hero in many of the retellings of the story. He became the subject of several stories and has emerged as a glorified hero.

so Kira's spies would not know they were planning a vendetta. On a wintery night in 1703, they raided Kira's mansion in Edo, killed him, and decapitated him. Then, they laid his head at the temple grave of Asano at Sengaku-ji. The *ronin* surrendered to the authorities after completing their revenge. Since they committed a capital crime, the shogunate ordered the *ronin* to commit *seppuku*. Several months later, all forty-seven committed *seppuku* on the same day. Their remains are also interred at Sengaku-ji. This account is known as the Ako Incident.

Scene from Chushingura - 47 *ronin*

Scene from Chushingura (Forty-seven ronin)

The fictionalized version is *Chushingura* (*The Treasury of Loyal Retainers*). *Chushingura* is actually based on a story in the fourteen-century chronicle, the *Taiheiki,* four centuries before the Ako Incident. However, the characters in *Chushingura* resemble those in the Ako Incident, and there are many other similarities. Some say the playwrights injected elements of a contemporary event (the Ako Incident) to make the old fictional story more dramatic. Others say the many similarities show it was a thinly disguised portrayal of the Ako Incident to avoid the shogunate ban on showing any events involving the samurai in the theater.

The story of *Chushingura* has been told in kabuki, *bunraku* (puppet play), stage plays, novels, movies, television shows, and other media. There have been at least a half dozen novels on the subject and over ten television versions. Though these books and productions are based on a real event, the facts have been embellished and dramatized. In prewar Japan, the most popular format was the Kabuki play, which was first performed in 1748. At that time, the fictional *Chushingura* became famous, while the real Ako Incident was little known. As a result, people began to believe that what was in the play really happened historically. Later versions of the play changed the setting from the fourteenth century to the eighteenth century to coincide with the time of the Incident and began using the names of the real Ako characters. Today, this is how the *Chushingura* story is presented in films and television. The real Ako Incident has been fused with the fictional *Chushingura* story.

In the postwar era, the most popular media was films, with at least seven film versions of *Chushingura*. Even Hollywood joined with its fantasy adaptation, *47 Ronin* (2013). But the most prolific medium has been television dramas. It started in 1964 with the NHK historical drama *Ako Roshi*, based on the 1927 novel by Osaragi Jiro, followed by at least twenty-one television shows about *Chushingura*. *Chushingura* continues to be of interest because people believe it is based on an actual historical event. The mythical image of the samurai willing to sacrifice his life for loyalty and justice continues to persist—it is embedded in Japanese thinking after countless exposures to the story.

There is criticism of the glorification of *Chushingura*. Much of it relates to the crux of the story, the concept of *chushin gishi* (loyal and dutiful samurai). It is the fundamental element of Bushido, where loyalty to the lord is the highest and most sacred obligation. Some say people who had given their lives for a greater cause deserve veneration. Others would go even further and push for deification. In modern times, the Yasukuni Shrine in Tokyo, a shrine dedicated to the war dead, honored those who followed *chushin gishi* and gave their lives for a noble purpose. It has become a center of controversy. *Chushin gishi* could be interpreted as unquestioning loyalty to the master or higher authorities and could lead to fanaticism, resulting in malicious behavior and becoming an excuse to engage in criminal activities.

It comes down to the question of motive. The readiness of the samurai to demonstrate loyalty did not mean they were nonthinking retainers who automatically responded. The samurai followed the precept of *makoto* (sincerity or truthfulness). Ivan Morris viewed *makoto* as an essential quality of the samurai hero. The samurai's actions should show "purity of motive." Furthermore, a righteous motive should characterize all participants, so if the superior has an unrighteous motive, the bond of loyalty is broken.[67]

Loyalty in *chushin gishi* is a two-way proposition. The retainer's livelihood is dependent on the lord, so the retainer extends abiding loyalty to protect this dependency. The motivation is one of self-preservation. The lord, in turn, needs the services of the retainer to maintain his territory. He is obligated to protect and reward his retainer when necessary. It is a mutually dependent relationship, but the lord has more leverage as the commanding authority. What if he decides to pursue his self-interest at the expense of the retainer? This troubling situation happened in the Sengoku period when perpetual warfare created instability and chaos that led a few lords to seek their self-interest.

Unusual situations occurred with subordinates overthrowing their superiors. It is a phenomenon called *gekokujo* (lower overthrowing the upper). During Sengoku, the social order was in flux, and constant changes created opportunities for social mobility. Some feudal lords advanced their position based on personal ambition to the detriment of the subordinate retainers. Their treacherous acts undermined loyalty. Retainers felt little loyalty to their lord when he acted immorally, so they overthrew him on moral principles. Sometimes, samurai moved from extreme loyalty to extreme disobedience simply out of a moral sense of doing the right thing. However, the act of *gekokujo* was limited because treachery and disloyalty were the concerns of only the upper levels of the samurai class, and the lower levels and the peasantry were not directly involved.

The military diluted the myth of absolute loyalty in modern times. During the 1930s, repeated acts of *gekokujo* occurred when young army officers of the Imperial Way Faction disobeyed the wishes of the general staff and attempted the assassination of public figures. Junior officers of

---

67 See Morris, *The Nobility*, for extended discussion of makoto.

the Japanese Kwantung Army in Manchuria exercised *gekokujo* when they defied the orders from the Imperial General Headquarters in Tokyo and took autonomous actions. It led to the Mukden Incident 1931, which resulted in the Japanese invasion of Manchuria. For their actions, the young officers received light sentences because the Japanese public was supportive of their *makoto,* their sincerity or purity of motive. Yet these actions done supposedly for the emperor were a far cry from Kusunoki obediently following the direct orders of Emperor Go-Daigo. The problem with motives is you can be doing the wrong activities for the right reasons. The Japanese extreme nationalists and the junior officers had the right reasons, serving the emperor and the high purposes of Japan. But assassinations and aggression against foreign countries were absolutely wrong—they were the wrong actions for the right reason. It is interesting to note that modern-day Japanese extremists, the left-wing Japanese "Red Army" and the right-wing Shield Society of Yukio Mishima, both cited *makoto* and the example of the mythical samurai. Unfortunately, this was the self-destructive path of *makoto.*[68]

What happens when the loyalty tie between a samurai and his feudal lord is severed? The samurai becomes a *ronin.* In the Sengoku period, it was a common occurrence with the death of the *daimyo* or the clan's destruction in battle. But it could happen for other reasons, for example, the disgrace of the lord or the samurai's dismissal. The samurai could leave his family, relatives, and master for personal reasons, then becomes a wandering warrior looking for employment. Several movies use the roaming *ronin* as a trope. Indeed it became the standard. The *Seven Samurai* (1954), *Yojimbo* (1961), and *Sanjuro* (1962), three films directed by Akira Kurosawa, use the theme of a *ronin* or a group of *ronin.* These films dramatically altered the image of the traditional samurai. He no longer was pure, simple, and clean-cut. Moreover, the films had an international appeal and impacted the cinematic world. In Chapter Two, in the section on Revision and Demythologization, the influence of these films was discussed. An American version of *Seven Samurai* was produced, and *Yojimbo,* in particular, was copied by the spaghetti Westerns.

---

68 Turnbull, *Lone Samurai,* 152-53.

Akira Kurosawa

In the movies, the ronin or his band would travel the countryside. Whenever a situation of gross power abuse was encountered, he or his band would step in and depose the criminal gang, thus saving the lives of the villagers. The films are based on factual background, and it is true this period is historically noted for its violence and chaos. But most *ronin* did not wander for long because they found employment and obviously did not have such a high-minded purpose. The characters and plots are fictitious and exaggerated but make for engaging storytelling. The virtue of loyalty was singled out from the war tales of the thirteenth and fourteenth centuries and became essential to the samurai myth. Later, it was enshrined in the Bushido code and developed into an ingrained ideal, a part of the samurai psyche. Today, most Japanese no longer glorify loyalty but they honor it. Loyalty is not the overarching virtue anymore because mitigating factors could undermine loyalty.

Myth: Honor is more important than life

For the samurai, life is transient, short and quick. He must be ready to meet death at any time. His attitude towards death and the manner in which he meets death is of utmost importance.

Sakura (cherry blossom) is associated with the samurai. In Japan, the blossoming of the cherry trees marks the arrival of spring. The delicate pink and white flowers last briefly for about a week to ten days, then fall and scatter. During periods of samurai dominance, from the Kamakura to the Edo period, the Japanese wrote about how the *sakura* reminded them of the warrior. Kabuki theater used this association in its dramas. A well-known proverb that originated in the medieval period states:

> *Hana wa sakuragi, hito wa bushi.*
> (The [best] blossom is the cherry blossom, the [best] man is the warrior)[69]

Sakura embodies the notion of renewal, for in spring, there is a burst of life, and then the beauty of the flowers takes over. But it soon ends with the falling of the petals. Similarly, the samurai appears ready to perform his duty; he personifies beauty with loyalty, honor, integrity, and self-discipline, and there is an acceptance of the impermanence of life. As the *sakura's* blossoms fade quickly, so too could the samurai's life abruptly end.

Life's impermanence teaches the samurai to seize the moment. How does the samurai respond? If he is victorious in battle, there is no problem, but if he suffers defeat and is still alive, a decision has to be made, and surrender is not an option. According to Yamaga Soko (1622-1685), scholar, military strategist, and philosopher of the Edo period: "Honor must be considered more important than life." A sense of personal honor is one of the virtues in the Bushido, the codification to which, Yamaga made major contributions. In his writings, he emphasized that one of the functions of the samurai is to be a behavior model.[70] In defeat, the samurai must not surrender because surrendering is a dishonorable act. *Seppuku* is the only option.

---

69 Daniel Crump Buchanan, ed., *Japanese Proverbs and Sayings* (Norman, OK: University of Oklahoma Press, 1965), 119. The Japanese military used the proverb during World War II.

70 David M. Earl, "Yamaga Soko," in vol. 8 *Kodansha Encyclopedia of Japan* (Tokyo: Kodansha, 1983), 290.

Yamaga Soko

Seppuku ritual

Reenactment of seppuku ritual

Disembowelment or *seppuku* is ritual suicide, and its origin is obscure. It occurred first in the tenth or eleventh century in the Minamoto clan of northern Japan. By the fourteenth century, the practice had spread to all of Japan but was limited to the samurai class. It is a slow and agonizing way to die. At first, it was used as capital punishment, as seen in the Ako Incident, where the forty-seven *ronin* were treated as criminals and ordered to commit *seppuku*. Only later, were they posthumously recognized as tragic heroes.

In the ritual suicide, a short sword is used with the initial cut made left to right across the abdomen. Why the stomach? Japanese believe the stomach is where the soul resides. Besides, it is where action and tension take place. There is a Japanese expression, *"hara ga tatsu"* ("the abdomen stands up"), which means one is angry and shows where the emotion comes from. In contrast, Americans believe the heart embodies the moral and emotional nature of human beings. Words such as "heartache," "heartfelt," and "heart-to-heart" point to the heart as the source of our feelings and emotions. Americans refer to the bowels as the soul of our feelings in such words as "gutless" and "gut-wrenching." Therefore, in some respects, Americans agree with the Japanese that the stomach is the source of our moral and emotional feelings. The Japanese prefer to start lower and then move up.

Since death is not immediate, the cut is continued upward. Over a period of time, the ritual evolved to where a *kaishakunin* (decapitation assistant) was employed to decapitate the head with one swing of the long sword. When the samurai makes the second cut upward, the body and head usually jerk forward, and this is the signal to decapitate the head. If done properly, it would cut short the agonizing pain. In the ceremonial *seppuku*, everything is planned. There are witnesses, the condemned person is properly dressed, weapons are arranged, and on occasion, a death poem or letter is written. Of course, under battlefield conditions, all rituals are set aside.

A *seppuku* ceremony was witnessed by the British diplomat Sir Ernest Mason Satow, who wrote about it in detail. The condemned samurai had ordered weapons to be fired on foreigners. He was sentenced to die and given a chance to meet death honorably.[71] Having witnesses is comparable to the Western practice of inviting witnesses to public executions.

As previously stated, *seppuku* was first used as punishment for criminal acts committed by the samurai. By the Edo period, its use was systematized to penalize disgraced samurai who had violated the

---

71 Ernest Mason Satow, *A Diplomat in Japan* (London: Seeley, Service & Co. Ltd., 1921), 345-46.

Bushido code. The samurai was to confront death honorably, thus redeeming his act. There are two other basic reasons for committing disembowelment—*junshi,* the self-immolation of a retainer following the death of his lord, and *seppuku,* used as a form of protest.

When *junshi* first happened in Japan is not known, but it is a practice that has taken place in China since ancient times. When the Chinese emperor died, his attendants were buried with the emperor to care for him in the other world. Since the attendants did not commit suicide, this practice doesn't fit our definition of *junshi.* In Japan, when the warriors first appeared in the tenth century, it was not uncommon for the retainers to commit suicide if their lord was killed in battle. But if the lord died of natural causes, *junshi* did not take place. In the Edo period, with no warfare, samurai began to follow their lord into death even though the lord may have died of illness or natural causes. These acts of suicide were considered to be the ultimate expression of their loyalty and gratitude for the lord's benevolence. Since a number of retainers were involved, multiple suicides resulted, but how many depended on the closeness of the relationship with the lord.

Tokugawa Ieyasu disliked *junshi* but allowed it to continue. It was considered a virtue, and those committing suicide were honored and interred near their lord, and their families were given benefits. The favors granted to the families induced more *junshi* to occur. An increase in *junshi* meant the loss of talented men, which was an increasingly critical problem, but more disconcerting was that *junshi* was performed for questionable reasons. Some did it because others were doing it, and they had no choice but to join. In other words, they did it out of obligation rather than loyalty. Just as troubling were those who did it for the benefits their descendants would receive, an act devoid of any sense of loyalty to the deceased lord.

With mounting criticism, the Tokugawa shogunate finally banned the custom of *junshi* in 1663. Thus, a custom in practice from the Sengoku to the early Edo period ended. Once the ban was instituted, there was only one violation, the Ako Incident. Although treated by the Tokugawa shogunate as criminals, the retainers acted for the right reason of loyalty to their lord. Their suicides were considered a form of *junshi.*

In the modern period, there has been only one case of *junshi* for the right reason of loyalty to the lord, in this case, the emperor. General Nogi Maresuke and his wife Shizuko committed *junshi* on September 13, 1912, the day of Emperor Meiji's funeral. They sat in front of the imperial portrait in their home and died by ritual suicide, following their emperor into death. Nogi disemboweled himself with a sword, and she stabbed herself in the heart with a dagger.[72] In his suicide letter, Nogi wished to make amends for the vast casualties suffered at Port Arthur during the Russo-Japanese War of 1904-05 and other military mistakes. He was already a national hero, so his *junshi* created a sensation and controversy. Some praised it as a heroic act, showing loyalty and purity of heart, while others condemned it as a backward act that hindered Japan as a modern nation. Nogi's *junshi* had such notoriety that it was the subject of novels by two famous writers, Mori Ogai (*The Abe Family*, 1913) and Soseki Natsume (*Kokoro*, 1914). Ogai in his stories is sympathetic with the practice of *junshi* and believed in the timeless features of the Japanese national character and thinking.[73] In contrast, Soseki agreed with the belief that each age has different values, and it is difficult to understand the thinking from one generation to another. What is proper in one period is no longer relevant in another and Japan has to move on.[74] In prewar films with Nogi as the theme, such as Yoshimura Misao's *Remember General Nogi! (1934)*, he is depicted as a grieving general anguished over the lost of his men. Without revealing his identity, Nogi visits the graves and comforts the surviving families. These prewar *jidaigeki* (period dramas) films promoted personal sacrifices as part of the nationalistic ideology, linking the lower classes with the military in a common fight to defend Japan. The draftee and his family must accept the sacrifices in carrying out the duty to protect the emperor. In postwar Japan, Nogi was portrayed in the 1980 film *The Battle of Port Arthur* with a different focus; no longer was it on the sacrifices to defend the ruler

---

72 Carol Gluck, *Japan's Modern Myths: Ideology in the Late Meiji Period* (Princeton, NJ: Princeton University Press, 1985), 221.

73 For a detailed analysis on the subject of death and the *junshi* of Gen. Nogi and the reaction to his death by Mori Ogai, see Robert Jay Lifton, Shuichi Kato and Michael R. Reich, *Six Lives, Six Deaths: Portraits from Modern Japan* (New Haven: Yale University Press, 1979), 29-66, 73-74. An in-depth study of the reactions of Ogai and Soseki to Nogi's junshi is Doris G. Bargen, *Suicidal Honor: General Nogi and the Writings of Mori Ogai and Natsume Soseki,* (Honolulu: University of Hawai'i Press, 2006).

74 Roy Starrs, "Writing the National Narrative: Changing Attitudes toward Nation-Building among Japanese Writers, 1900-1930," in Sharon A. Minichiello, ed. *Japan's Competing Modernities: Issues in Culture and Democracy, 1900-1930* (Honolulu, University of Hawai'i Press, 1998), 211-13.

as the highest form of ethical virtue. Instead, the emphasis was on the heroics of the battles. The preoccupation with Nogi continued, and he was the subject of an NHK television series, which aired from 2009 to 2011.

General Nogi Maresuke

Besides using *seppuku* as an expression of loyalty to one's superior and as a way to follow the superior in death, it could be used as a form of protest. To prevent the use of *junshi* for all such purposes, the Meiji government banned it, and except for the Nogi episode, it completely stopped after the nineteenth century. But surprisingly, it occurred again, as a form of protest in an unusual event, the coup attempt by the controversial novelist Mishima Yukio (1925-1970).

Several writers have committed suicide and explained how they were going to do it in their work. So, it was not unusual that Mishima wrote about it, but how he did it was dramatic. In the 1960s, he advocated for the right-wing cause, demanding political power be bestowed to the emperor and the military. On November 25, 1970, Mishima led four members of the Shield Society, his paramilitary organization, to attempt a coup. They took over the Eastern Command office of the commanding general of the Self Defense Force and tied the general to a chair. Then Mishima went to the balcony and delivered a speech to the assembled soldiers. The soldiers jeered and yelled, and Mishima concluded by shouting three times: "Long Live the Emperor." He returned to the room and proceeded with the ritual suicide. After executing the two cuts into the belly, the *kaishakunin* (decapitation assistant) was supposed to decapitate him but could not do it properly and instead committed *seppuku*. Another accomplice, who was versed in swordsmanship, promptly stepped in and decapitated Mishima. He then decapitated the *kaishakunin*.

Yukio Mishima

Mishima believed his purposes were high-minded, for he was protesting the decadent Western culture that had overtaken Japan. He wanted to revive the military culture and the samurai spirit. It was a matter of honor to carry out this task, even if it meant death. He was obsessed with death, and in his works, especially his photography, he showed and described death in all of its manifestations. The glorification and the fascination with dying are part of the ethos of the mythical samurai. In a nation noted for its high suicide rates and historical associations with acts of ritual suicide, it is a legacy that should be left completely behind, but it has not ceased. The Japanese public was unsympathetic towards Mishima's actions, and many abhorred such anachronistic behavior.

When *junshi* was the prevailing practice, it undermined the ethical codes of the clans and that of the developing Bushido. The precept that honor is more important than life originated from the codes. But when is *seppuku* appropriate, and how do you determine intent? Already, it was being done for inappropriate reasons. For the samurai, it created a moral dilemma—is the family to be sacrificed for the clan's honor? The authorities faced the same question.

The moral ambiguity and its consequences are starkly shown in the movie *Harakiri* (1962), directed by Kobayashi Masaki. The story takes place in the early Edo period and follows Tsugumo Hanshiro, a *ronin*, who comes to the *daimyo's* residence requesting permission to commit *seppuku*. The officials believe this is a ploy to gain pity and a job. He is told the story of another *ronin*, Chijiiwa Motome, who arrived a year ago asking to commit *seppuku*. But the officials believed he was bluffing, expecting to be turned away and given money. The three top officials of the clan decided to punish this *ronin*. They persuaded the senior retainer to order immediate *seppuku,* denying the plea of Motome for a couple of days' delay so he could settle matters with his family, who were suffering from illness. The officials forced him to commit *seppuku* with his bamboo sword—he had sold his swords to pay medical bills. Death by disembowelment with a bamboo blade is exceedingly painful and humiliating. Hanshiro denies knowing anything about Motome and asks to proceed with his ritual suicide. When asked to name his *kaishakunin,* he names the three officials who had coerced the suicide of Motome. Everyone is shocked, and Hanshiro tells the whole story. The coerced Motome is his son-in-law, and his death caused his grandson to die from his illness and his daughter to commit suicide. His entire family is destroyed. Hanshiro reveals that he had already confronted the three officials and had cut off their topknots. Fighting ensues, and Hanshiro kills four and wounds eight of the *daimyo's* retainers. Hanshiro is finally cornered, commits *seppuku* and is shot simultaneously by three retainers firing their muskets. Nevertheless, Hanshiro has his revenge. Of the three top officials, one immediately commits *seppuku,* and the other two are forced to commit suicide because they lost their topknots, a serious violation of clan rules. The final scenes show the elaborate suit of armor on display that was damaged in the fighting is now repaired, and the daily record book of the clan is read, listing two *seppuku* and several deaths by natural causes. The message is clear—there is hypocrisy on the part of the authorities, and the codes are a sham. Even so, the samurai tradition, as symbolized by the repaired armor suit, continues with all of its grandeur.

The film is regarded as anti-samurai. It came out almost two decades after the war. Already, there was mounting criticism about the mythical samurai. The samurai was not so virtuous, and often, injustices were covered up by codes and clan rules. A similar reaction occurred in the US against the mythical cowboy in the postwar era. The spaghetti western was a reaction to the staid prewar cowboy. Identical to the US, Japanese revisionism took off. In 2011, *Hara-Kiri: Death of a Samurai,* a 3D version of Kobayashi's film, was released. It was directed by Miike Takashi, and the remake was done in a spectacular fashion. The mythical samurai and cowboy did not disappear, but each was transformed into a modified figure. For the modified samurai, honor remained an essential virtue, but it could be mitigated and was no longer more important than life.

Myth: Samurai were orderly and skilled in killing and were cultured warriors

The samurai was a paradox in several ways, and this myth has puzzled and intrigued many experts and the general public. The myth is true but must be understood for its nuances. Here in this discussion, the contradictions are not resolved but are clarified.

Under conditions of incessant warfare, bands of samurai were insufficient, so local standing armies developed. Over time, there were changes in tactics, strategies, and customs. In the beginning, fighting was localized on a smaller scale, and conventions and traditions were followed. Warfare was fighting between rival samurai families and clans; it was a battle between elites, not a battle with commoners or between commoners. There were no conscript armies. Fighting was like a sporting competition with limited scope and highly ritualized. Armies fought on open fields or flat lands, avoiding hilly terrains and mountains. Horses were the principal means of movement, and open fields were ideal. Contrary to the image of the samurai as warriors on foot fighting with the sword, samurai were on horseback, and their weapon was the long bow (*yumi*), not the long sword (*katana*). The long bow was about seven feet long and made of a composite of wood and bamboo. Commoners were the foot soldiers (*ashigaru*) and were primarily armed with spears (*yari*) and halberds, which were long poles with curved blades (*naginata*). Therefore, the weapons that were carried differed according to the rank of the combatants, and the outfits were strikingly different. The higher-status samurai were fully armored and wore elaborate helmets (*kabuto*) with ornaments. They often wore gargoyle-like face masks, designed to frighten the enemy by their fierce appearance. On the other hand, the foot soldiers had little armor and wore war hats (*jingasa*) conical helmets without ornaments.

Samurai with weapons
L. to r: weapons are halberd, long bow, and spear

Samurai with weapons
L to r: halberd, long bow, and spear.

The battle began with the armies in formation facing each other. Each side had colorful banners proclaiming the families and clans involved. The leader would stand in front of his army and, in a loud voice, give his name, announce his lineage or ancestry, and tell of his deeds of heroism in battles. In response, the leader of the opposing army would step forward and give his challenge. After the exchange, the leaders would return to their respective formations, and a special arrow with a hollow shaft would be shot, giving a whizzing sound, the signal for the fighting to begin. First, a volley of arrows would be fired, followed by a charge with samurai on horseback leading the way. A phrase often used was "*kyuba no michi*" ("way of horse and bow"), an indication of the elite status of the mounted samurai archers and their prowess. The bow was considered a long-range weapon compared to the sword or spear. A target could be hit at thirty yards. Hand-to-hand combat came at the final stage, and the sword became important, but at times, the fighting ended before it reached this stage. Close combat did not always happen.

The conventions of warfare were clearly laid out and meant to make warfare more civil; however, there were occasions when procedures were violated. This is not surprising since wars throughout the world have experienced violations of established combat norms. Even so, the conventions were the accepted standard, and no significant changes occurred in the rules and conduct of warfare until the thirteenth century. The impetus for change came from a foreign threat, not domestic development.

The Mongols under Kublai Khan invaded Japan in 1274 and again in 1281. Both times, the weather intervened and disrupted the Mongol invaders. The typhoon was especially devastating in the second attempt, and the Mongol fleet was demolished. Japanese attributed the destruction of the Mongol fleet to a divine intervention caused by *kamikaze* (divine wind). Japanese suicide pilots in World War II adopted the word as their title and became *kamikaze* pilots.

In terms of the battles with the Mongols, the samurai could contain them on the beaches, but they found their conventions of warfare useless. There was no common language or communication with the foreign invaders. When the Japanese leader stepped out and offered his challenge, the Mongol leader did not step out. Instead, he ordered the attack. Rather than a single humming arrow to commence battle, the Mongols launched volleys of arrows, accompanied by drums and battle cries, sounds the Japanese had never heard. The Mongols advanced in a phalanx formation with shields held high to fend off arrows. It was a new formation the Japanese had never faced before, but they made the necessary adjustments. As a result of their experiences with the Mongols, the Japanese adopted the use of battle cries. Before a battle, the samurai shouted out "*ei, ei, o*" (pronounced "ay, ay, oh"), getting louder with each repeat. Drums were also used before and during the battle. The practice of the leader stepping out and introducing himself and hurling challenges was gradually dispensed with as armies grew larger and warfare became less personalized.

Still, the fighting was personal enough that the samurai had a strong desire to know who they were killing. They had to show proof they killed the right person. After the battle, severed heads were collected and identified. If there was time after the battle, further identification was made by markers placed on the upper lip and nose or a tag attached to the hair to distinguish the victim. The headhunt was needed to verify the individual accomplishment of the samurai, and based on the headcount, it could lead to an increase in stipend or promotion. Women cleaned the severed heads and applied light cosmetics to make them presentable. It was a way to pay respect to the dead. Some samurai were concerned about the presentability of their heads after their death. They placed incense inside their helmet in case they were killed so their head would not be odorous and bother their killer. After the cleaning, the final step was to hold a *kubi jikken* (head-viewing inspection). It was presented before the lord, and each head was offered for his inspection. This was a gruesome ceremony, but it was made into a celebration with food and drinks served.

Head-viewing inspection (Kubi jikken)

One such event had disastrous results for those celebrating the head-viewing inspection. It occurred during the Battle of Okehazama in 1560, a decisive battle of the Sengoku period. The *daimyo* Imagawa Yoshimoto had advanced with a large army into Oda Nobunaga's territory. Yoshimoto's army was resting in a gorge when he ordered a celebration of *kubi jikken*. He viewed a parade of enemy heads from the armies they had decimated as they fought through the province. Each head had a label on the pigtail, declaring the name of the victim and the samurai who killed him. Everyone was having a good time; food was consumed, and sake flowed freely. Meanwhile, Nobunaga's men silently occupied the surrounding hills. At an opportune time, Nobunaga's small army attacked and surprised the unprepared Imagawa troops, who fled, leaving Yoshimoto's headquarters unprotected. Yoshimoto did not know what happened and thought his men had gotten into a drunken fight. He saw two men running towards him, and when he recognized the two as Nobunaga's warriors, it was too late. He wounded one of the men, but the other warrior grabbed him and chopped off his head. The two Nobunaga men became heroes. They had attained the highest prize in the headhunt—the head of the rival lord.

At times, head-hunting occurred under peculiar conditions. After some battles, peasants would look for stragglers of the defeated army. This practice of hunting for samurai who were no longer part of the retinue was *ochimusha-gari* (fallen warrior hunter). The peasants wanted the expensive swords and other equipment the samurai took from them. They hunted for the defeated warriors, killed them, and severed their heads. Then, they collected the swords, equipment, and the heads, for which they could receive bounties.

In modern times, the fascination with severed heads and head-hunting caused national confusion. Such was the case of Saigo Takamori's (1828-1877) head. Saigo led the Satsuma Rebellion in 1877, protesting against the Meiji government's abolishment of the samurai class, rice stipends, and other policies against the samurai traditions. He and his rebel army wanted to restore the honor of the samurai. In the early morning of September 24, 1877, the Battle of Shiroyama began. Saigo and his remnant army of three hundred were crushed by seven thousand imperial troops. How Saigo died is not known. One story says Saigo was severely wounded in the last suicide charge, and one of his aides cut off his head and hid it from the imperial troops to preserve his honor. Another source said he committed *seppuku,* but he could not have done this due to his hip wound and a shattered femur. And later, an autopsy revealed no wounds to the abdomen. There are conflicting reports on how Saigo's headless body laid on the battlefield, and who hid and found his head. However, there is a reliable account of how Saigo's head was rejoined with his body. John Capen Hubbard, an American ship captain working for the Mitsubishi Steamship Company to transport government troops and supplies, wrote to his wife about the battle scene. He could tell it was Saigo's body because of its size. Saigo was larger in stature than the average Japanese. According to Hubbard, someone brought his head and placed it by the body. Such a report was suppressed, and most Japanese did not hear about this eyewitness report; even today, it is not public knowledge. The Japanese public was not willing to accept such an account—how could their legendary hero have such an inglorious ending, lying naked with a severed head?[75]

Saigo Takamori

---

75 Mark Ravina, *The Last Samurai: The Life and Battles of Saigo Takamori* (Hoboken, NJ: John Wiley & Sons, Inc., 2004), 211-12.

Artists know how the story should end. They knew what the Japanese people wanted. Soon, *nishikie* (woodblock prints) were published showing the presentation of Saigo's head and his associates' heads to Yamagata Aritomo (1838-1922), the commander of the imperial army and his counterpart representing the emperor. The prints were entitled *"kubi jikken"* ("inspection of heads"), an obvious reference to the old samurai tradition of head-viewing. The Meiji government had already banned the feudal practice of displaying heads, so the prints were not based on a factual event, but it did not matter because the general public got what it wanted.[76]

In 1897, the most lasting myth about Saigo's head was developed by Kawasaki Saburo. In this story, Saigo's head is presented to Yamagata for inspection. Yamagata treated the head with great respect. Before becoming a rebel, Saigo held important positions and was one of the most powerful men in the Meiji government. Yamagata and Saigo were colleagues, having fought together to overthrow the Tokugawa shogunate. All of these events he recalled as he slowly and tenderly inspected the severed head. Yamagata washed the head in clean water. Then, holding it high in both hands, he turned to the assembled commanders and spoke of Saigo's last moments. He pointed out how Saigo's expression is calm even in the face of death. Then Yamagata wept for his fellow warrior. It is a poignant scene, a fitting ending for a tragic hero.[77]

This imaginative account became a source for building the Saigo Takamori myth. He was a samurai of humble origins, and a rebel leader who went against the Meiji government and died for a lost cause. Nevertheless, he became a national hero. Even before his death, he was revered and transformed into a demigod. This was the beginning of the apotheosis of Saigo. It is comparable to the apotheosis of Lincoln and Washington. Woodblock prints showed him as ascending into heaven and looking down on Japan. When a comet passed over Southern Japan in August 1877, it was reported that an image of Saigo was seen in the comet through the telescope. Newspapers fully covered Saigo's association with heavenly bodies—he was transformed into a celestial being.

---

76 Ravina, *Last Samurai*, 212 .
77 Ravina, 212-213.

Saigo's image continues in present-day Japan. The well-known novelist Shiba Ryotaro wrote *Tobu ga gotoku* (*As If in Flight*), a historical novel about Saigo. It was made into a NHK taiga drama with forty-eight episodes in 1990.[78] However, a more imposing memorial is a huge bronze statue of Saigo in Tokyo's Ueno Park. Unlike the famous statue of Kusunoki on the Imperial Palace grounds, Saigo's statue is without the full warrior regalia of helmet, armor, and weapons. Instead, he is in casual attire, only has one short sword, wearing sandals, and his dog is on a leash. He is not mounted on a horse; except for the short sword, there is nothing to show that he was a samurai.

Statue of Saigo Takamori, Ueno Park

Takamori's statue in Ueno Park

Kusunoki and Saigo were tragic samurai warriors, heroes who were on the losing side and died on the battlefield. Over the years, this outward image of the heroic samurai was altered. He is infrequently portrayed as a killing machine with all the trappings. The emphasis is less on his fighting skills, reflecting on how combat changed. It evolved from individualized actions to massive anonymous engagements. Fighting tactics, customs, and traditions were modified. Even the victory celebration with the head-viewing ceremony became distasteful

---

78 Taiga drama (big river drama) is the name Nihon Hoso Kyokai (NHK), a public service network, gave to its annual year-long historical drama. It began in 1963. Each weekly episode lasts for forty-five minutes. Many of the series are based on historical novels.

and was abandoned. What did not change were the inward virtues and values held by the samurai, such as courage and a sense of duty. These are still honored and respected. The outward myth of the samurai as a skilled and orderly fighter is no longer appropriate, and the skills, rituals and customs associated with the samurai became outmoded.

But what about the other side of the myth—was the samurai a cultured warrior? Was he a practitioner and advocate of literature and the arts? From the earliest days of the development of the samurai, literary (*bun*) arts were considered complementary to the military (*bu*) arts. Slogans such as "the twin ways of the literary and military arts" (*bunbu ryodo*) clarified the importance of both. The household laws of the *daimyo* instructed the samurai to cultivate the literary and military arts. Further refinement of the balance between literature and that of war was stated in the Households Laws of the Tokugawa (*Buke shohatto*) of 1615: "From of old the rule has been to practice 'the arts of peace on the left hand, and the arts of war on the right;' both must be mastered."[79]

The Influence of the literary arts on the samurai came from two sources: the Chinese literati and the courtiers in Kyoto. The samurai tried to copy the works and practices of the Chinese literati, that is, the mandarin (public officials) and the gentry class. The samurai were the closest counterpart to the role played by the Chinese officials. When the samurai largely replaced the courtiers in the Kyoto court in the twelfth century, it became easier to imitate the aristocratic court officials.

The samurai had a high level of education, and experts say they were better educated than European knights. This background gave the samurai the ethos and skills appropriate for official careers in the government and imperial court and provided them with access to Chinese literary works. Many could read Chinese texts, and soon, they were writing and composing poems in the Chinese style. Three art forms showed Chinese influence and were closely associated with each other: calligraphy, poetry, and painting. Of these, the upper-class samurai distinguished themselves in calligraphy and poetry.

---

79 Henry Smith, ed., *The Learning from Shogun: Japanese History and Western Fantasy* (Santa Barbara, CA: Program in Asian Studies, University of California, Santa Barbara, 1980), 90.

Calligraphy (*shodo*) is more than the skillful writing of Chinese characters; the writing can be aesthetically enjoyed.[80] It was considered an essential learning for any cultured person, such as the samurai. Excellence in writing was believed to reveal the inner character. Mastery of writing with brush (*fude*) and Chinese ink (*sumi*) developed the samurai's moral stature. As the saying goes: "You practice writing the characters to develop your character."

Poetry developed along with calligraphy. During the Heian period, all Japanese poetry was written in Chinese and done in this style. The Japanese assiduously studied and copied Chinese examples, and soon, the samurai court officials began to compose poetry. In the fourteenth century, during the Kamakura period, the Japanese language developed to a level where they began to write in their own language. Nevertheless, the Chinese influence was still present and, in fact, was revived when Zen monks returned from their trips to China.

When the samurai replaced the courtiers and became patrons of the arts, their preferences and tastes determined, to some extent, the directions taken by artisans. Aesthetic taste developed at this time, and there was heightened interest in such activities as the tea ceremony (*chanoyu*), flower arrangement (*ikebana*), cultivation of miniature trees (*bonsai*), and the No drama.[81] These cultural activities went beyond the court into the provinces and were enjoyed by many others in feudal society. Especially significant was the role played by Zen Buddhism with its focus on meditation, which created a wide interest in the tea ceremony, calligraphy, ink-painting (*sumi-e*), and landscape gardening. Why would the samurai, a warrior by profession, be interested in sitting through a tea ceremony and viewing some rock formations jutting out from gravel? In part, the aesthetic appreciation and meditative aspects were attractive because they allowed the samurai respite from society's stresses and strains. In the absence of warfare, there were opportunities to break away from the pace of life in the increasingly congested castle town and enjoy the contemplative aspects of the arts. Moreover, the

---

80 Early calligraphic writings are considered works of art, and today they are in demand by collectors and have become expensive.

81 In particular, chanoyu had a profound impact on samurai life. Sen no Rikyu, the Buddhist monk who played an important part in the development of chanoyu, was the tea master for Nobunaga and Hideyoshi. Chanoyu was a major event for the ruing elites.

meditative nature of the arts helped in the discipline of one's emotional and behavioral thoughts and actions.

Historical chronicles dominated the prose literature of the feudal period. However, some historical and war tales and other writings placed emphasis on the human and the dramatic rather than a mere narrative of events. In the well-known *Heike Monogatari* (*The Tale of the Heike*), there are accounts of samurai leaders and their intrigues and tragic deaths. In these stories we learn of Yoshitsune, the tragic hero. Later in the *Taiheiki* (*Record of Great Peace*), there are not only accounts of fighting but poems, anecdotes, Buddhist precepts, and so forth. The story about Kusunoki appears in this historical epic. These works were referenced by dramatists and writers in their plays and books. The tales were acted out in Noh, a dance-drama, and *kyogen*, a comic act. Noh dances were highly stylized; actors wore masks, accompanied by a chorus, flute, and drums. It appealed to the samurai class. Kyogen, on the other hand, appealed to the commoners with its slapstick and satire. It had no masks or chorus and used mockery and sarcasm with its simple plots. Popular dramas about the samurai were performed in Kabuki, a new form of theater presentation developed in the early Edo period. It featured stylized acting, singing, and dancing. The plots were from puppet plays, historical texts, or current events. In the latter case, if the story was politically sensitive, as it was with *Chushingura*, it was altered to avoid government censorship. The majority of dance-drama, stage, and puppet plays were based on epic historical accounts. It was the dance-drama Noh that the samurai found most interesting, and they became the patrons of Noh. Hence, the exploits and stories of the samurai were the subject matter of various literary works, and the tales were retold in dramas, dances, and theatrical performances. The samurai supported these artistic activities and in a few cases became patrons.

The Ashikaga shoguns were interested in Chinese paintings and promoted them. The Chinese influence was pervasive in the visual arts—in picture scroll (*emaki*), sculpture, and architecture. Slowly, Japanese themes and styles began to prevail among the samurai class. It was evident in the scrolls, which often depicted battle scenes, and covered a wide range of subjects, including religious themes, stories of prominent people, processions and ceremonies held at the palace, and so forth. The samurai had paintings done on screens and panels within their residences. In contrast, woodblock prints (*hanga*) were less expensive and more accessible to people in the rapidly growing urban centers. It was mass-produced and the most popular art form of the Tokugawa period. *Hanga* subjects included legendary warriors, Kabuki actors, landscapes, and courtesans. Woodblock prints became the best visual source of life in Tokugawa times.

The legacies of the samurai as patrons, connoisseurs, and practitioners of the arts continue to this day. The most poignant reminder of the samurai paradox as a fighting and cultured warrior was the role and behavior of the Japanese Imperial Army officers. Two examples show the paradox, one from the Russo-Japanese War of 1904-05 and the other from World War II.

First, let us examine General Nogi Maresuke as the example from the Russo-Japanese War. Governments honor heroes in many ways, with statues, memorial buildings, and their names affixed to parks, roadways, other geographical features, and man-made structures. One way the national government recognizes heroes is through the issuance of postage stamps. General Nogi Maresuke and other military leaders were honored in a series of stamps issued in the 1930s. Today, when the Japanese government acknowledges heroes, whether prewar or postwar, they are civilians—writers, educators, actors, artists, scientists, musicians, and so forth.[82] Even though defeat in World War II tarnished the Japanese military heroes, their legacies continue. General Nogi was featured on a postage stamp as a national hero for his exploits in the Russo-Japanese War. But today, he is noted as a hero because of his sense of loyalty and duty and an upholder of the samurai ideals. We have already discussed his controversial practice of *junshi*. Here, our focus is on his literary skills as a poet and the subjects of his poems, reflecting samurai virtues. He was a talented *kanshi* (poems in the Chinese language) poet, and the following poem, written in the midst of the Russo-Japanese War, was popular during the Meiji era:

---

82 John W. Dower, *Ways of Forgetting, Ways of Remembering: Japan in the Modern World* (New York: The New Press, 2012), 255, 306.

Mountains and rivers, trees and grass, have become
cold and desolate.
For ten *li*, the foul oder of blood drifts on the wind
over new battlefields.
My brave horse would not advance, and the soldiers
are silent.
I stand outside Jinzhou Town, in the setting sun.

The above poem was written outside the walls of Jinzhou after the
Battle of Nanshan of 1904, in which his eldest son was killed.

Nireisan was indeed difficult to climb,
But it was overcome by the deeds of young men.
Under a mantle of iron and blood, the mountain's
shape is changed.
Now all look up in awe at Nireisan.

This poem was written at Nireisan after the battle of Hill 203 of 1904-
05, where he lost his second son.

The Emperor's army, a million strong, set out to
punish the powerful savages of the north.

On the battlefield, in the midst of the sieges, the
bodies of the dead piled up like mountains.

I am ashamed to show my face to the fathers who
remain back home, though we few return today in
triumph.

The poem cited above was written just before Nogi's return to Japan
from Manchuria after the end of the war. He was always concerned
about the huge casualties suffered during the war, so he requested
permission from the emperor to atone for the casualties by committing
seppuku; but the emperor denied the request. Nogi had another outlet,
the *kanshi* poems. What prompted him to pen the poems was clearly
the dreadful wartime experiences, especially the deaths of his sons.
Despite the poems' association with the military, Nogi is respected
as a notable *kanshi* poet and remains popular among academics and
intellectuals.

Lieutenant General Kuribayashi Tadamichi is the second example. He was the commander of the Japanese garrison on Iwo Jima. In the desperate final battle on March 16, 1945, he sent a farewell telegram to the Imperial General Headquarters. Farewell telegrams are published in the newspapers, but the government could redact them, and in the case of Kuribayashi's telegram, it was redacted to protect public morale. But he added a *jisei* (a death poem in three stanzas) to the end of his message:

Unable to complete this heavy task for our country
Arrows and bullets all spent, so sad we fall.

But unless I smite the enemy,
My body cannot rot in the field.

Yea, I shall be born again seven times
And grasp the sword in my hand.

When ugly weeds cover this island,
My sole thought shall be the Imperial Land.[83]

Lt. Gen. Kuribayashi Tadamichi

---

83 Kumiko Kakehashi, *So Sad to Fall in Battle: An Account of War* (New York: Presidio Press, 2007), xxiii.

Traditionally, death poems are written to express love of country and loyalty to the emperor. In lines 5-6: "Yea, I shall be born again seven times / And grasp the sword in my hand" is originally from *Taiheki* and was used by the medieval hero Kusunoki. The desire to fight again and again for the emperor is a common theme from the days of the samurai, a continuation of the revere tradition of imperial loyalty.

In the modern age, the tradition of the samurai continued. Japanese commanders could be men of killing, allowing or ordering ruthless acts, such as the Rape of Nanking and the Bataan Death March; however, at the same time be men of culture, writing letters and poems. Both Nogi and Kuribayashi were cultured warriors but were troubled by leading a killing organization. The paradox of the samurai remains and has its consequences. In regards to this dichotomy, the sixteenth-century *daimyo*, Kuroda Nagamasa, wrote:

> The arts of peace and the arts of war are like the two wheels of a cart which, lacking one, will have difficulty in standing.[84]

Myth: The sword was the life of the samurai

In the beginning, this myth was not true. It only took hold when the nature of warfare changed in the early stages of feudalism. Once the alteration occurred, the sword became paramount and remained the primary weapon of the samurai until it was undermined by the introduction of firearms in the sixteenth century. The samurai wore two swords, a long sword (*katana*) and a short sword (*wakizashi*), and the combination is known as *daisho*. The sword remained a symbol of the samurai class until it was forbidden by the Meiji government in 1876.

When the samurai first appeared in history, the sword was not a weapon of importance. As alluded to previously, the image of the samurai fighting on foot with a sword is false. Woodblock prints, historical chronologies, and other writings always pictured the early samurai mounted on a horse, fully armored, and carrying a long bow. The bow was an effective long-range weapon, and the samurai were skilled in using it. It required long periods of practice to be proficient

---

84 Gregory M. Lee, ed., *Ideals of the Samurai: Writings of Japanese Warriors*, trans. and intro. William Scott Wilson (Santa Clarita, CA: Ohara Publications, 1982), 133.

with the bow while riding on a fast-moving horse. In training sessions called *yabusame,* the samurai would be upright in the saddle, turn sideway to clear the bow and shoot at the target while in a gallop. Today it is performed as a ritual and in special demonstrations.

On the battlefield, it was a harrowing experience for the enemy soldiers to see a line of mounted samurai charging with a fusillade of arrows in the air. Out of fright, the enemy usually retreated or ran in disarray. Consequently, with the enemy in full retreat, there was no need to use the sword, a weapon designed for close combat.

By the late fifteenth century, armies were larger and more complex. An increasing number of foot soldiers (ashigaru) were required as battle plans became sophisticated. Peasants were recruited on a temporary basis to supplement the *ashigaru.* Together, they formed the rank and file of the armies. Both *ashigaru* and peasants wore light or no armor and were armed with spears and halberds to dismount the samurai.

The mounted archers were still in vogue in the thirteenth century when the Mongol invasions took place, a defining moment in how battles were fought. With shields held high to deflect the arrows, phalanx formations employed by the Mongols undermined the effectiveness of the mounted archers. Moreover, the Mongols retaliated with volleys of arrows. Due to the change in tactics, close combats ensued, and to the surprise of the Japanese, their swords were of superior quality compared to those of the Mongols. There was a shift from cavalry warfare to infantry warfare. It signaled the decline of the mounted warrior. However, the possession of horses and swords continued to distinguish the high-ranking samurai from the lower classes. The sword became the symbolic "life" of the samurai.

The Japanese sword has become legendary. We are not talking about mass-produced military weapons but individually hand-produced swords. Bladesmithing is a refined art, and the Japanese workmanship is unsurpassed in the world. The formula and techniques are kept secret, and knowledge is transferred only to trusted apprentices.

The process of sword-making is laborious and time-consuming. The first stage is to harden a lump of steel and by hammering and folding it into a single plate. Then, it's notched or slitted, folded over, and heated to weld the surfaces tightly together. The process is repeated as many as thirty times, producing a multi-layered plate. This gives the blade tremendous strength and a sharp cutting edge. After further refinement, it is finally shaped and polished. The blade has a wavy line where the hard cutting edge meets the blade's body. The swordsmith's name, location, and date are etched on the tang of the blade into which the handle is inserted.[85]

In the early period, the mounted samurai carried a very long sword, the *tachi,* but because of its length, it had to be slung from a belt with its cutting edge facing downwards. Two hands were required to withdraw the sword from the scabbard, a difficult maneuver to do while riding a horse. However, the samurai had another shorter sword, the *katana,* which could be tucked in the belt, withdrawn in one long motion, and swung at the enemy. The *katana* became the preferred sword of the samurai.[86]

Stephen Turnbull, the samurai specialist, estimates there were as many as 3,550 swordsmiths in the fifteenth century, and an astounding thirty thousand swords were exported to other countries.[87] This is the mass production of a weapon that came to have symbolic value for the samurai. Obviously, these swords did not have the workmanship described above.

With the increase in swords came the necessity for training. In the fourteenth century, the first training establishment was founded. It was called *ryu,* a "school" of martial arts, but the meaning is that of a continuing tradition rather than a building. It is like a school of painting named for its style or its founder. In contrast, the Japanese word *dojo* denotes the practice hall or building where training is held.

One immediate problem was training or practicing with the sword without hurting or killing your partner. The *ryu* solved the problem by introducing the *bokuto,* wooden swords shaped like a real sword and heavy because of the dense wood, making its weight approximately that of a real sword. Even though it did not kill anyone, it still resulted in severe bruising. By the end of the sixteenth century, the *shinai* was developed, a light bamboo sword made of four bamboo slats held together by a leather sleeve, which, in the old style, could cover the

85 Turnbull, *Lone Samurai,* 38-40.
86 Turnbull, 40.
87 Turnbull, 40.

entire bamboo. In the modern *shinai*, the slats are held together by three leather fittings, one at the tip, another in the middle, and the third forming the hilt or handle. This is the practice sword used in present-day *kendo*, the Japanese sport of fencing. Since the *shinai* was light, there was a tendency to take many wild swings in practice, so a series of standard forms called *kata* was instituted. These fixed patterns are endlessly practiced in stylized fighting, where each partner could anticipate the other's next move. The fighting patterns developed by the Japanese have been copied and used in many countries. In the lightsaber combats of the *Star Wars* film, seven fighting styles were employed, which were derived and heavily influenced by Japanese martial arts, especially *kendo*.

The training and practice in using swords were not popularized until the Edo period. With no warfare, schools could have their lessons without interference and interruptions. In the previous Sengoku period, there was little time to train. Skills in using swords and other weapons had to be learned on the battlefields.

While the fighting styles are uniquely Japanese, the cinematic world has its interpretation of how dueling and sword combat should be shown. In prewar movies, the *chambara* (sword fighting) was a staged and stylized combat. There was no gushing of blood. When the victim was slashed, he would pirouette slowly to the ground. My favorite movie hero was a *ronin*, Tange Sazen. He always appeared immaculate in a white outfit (symbol of purity), had a cut over one eye, and fought with only one good arm, the result of an early betrayal. A typical scene would have him surrounded by a dozen men, and he would cut them down, one by one, until only half were left, and the remnant would promptly flee. Tange Sazen would then sheathe his sword and stroll nonchalantly down the street. Sword fights were carefully choreographed.

In comparison, the postwar *chambara* have an abundance of violence, and the gore is vividly portrayed. The fighting scenes are explicit and realistic in a movie like *Yojimbo*, directed by Akira Kurosawa. There are no dance-like scenes. It is actually how sword fighting occurred, bloody with lots of slicing. Swords utilized by Roman Legionnaires and medieval knights were double-edged blades employed in a plunging movement. In contrast, the *katana* is a single-edged weapon used to slice or cut, allowing for stylized motions. Even so, the postwar movies focused on brute strength not niceties.

Katana were often used as gifts and as offerings to the gods in Shinto shrines. The *katana* and its matching smaller sword were the exalted symbol of the samurai class. Besides being uniquely regarded as works of art, they had taken on an aura of authority and spirituality.

MYTH: Ninja were superhuman samurai

Japanese and American films built the image of the ninja as extraordinary fighters with mystical powers. The ninja myth could be likened to the fictional James Bond, the hero of many spy films. The lack of detailed information on the role played by the ninja allowed writers to create imaginative and romanticized stories. There is little mention of ninja in the historical chronicles because much of their assignments were clandestine, as in intelligence gathering and spying; hence, their activities were shrouded in secrecy.

Another term frequently used in lieu of ninja (invisible man) is *shinobi* (man of stealth). The meaning is basically the same, and they can be used interchangeably. However, there is a difference etymologically because *shinobi* was used much earlier. The British ninja historian Antony Cummins prefers *shinobi,* but American writers use ninja since they are unfamiliar with the word. Americans are also more familiar with the word *ninjutsu* (the art of stealth), which is associated with the ninja.

During incessant warfare, there was a need to conduct espionage activities against rival warlords. Ninja were employed to obtain information about the opposition's plans and operations using the technique of *ninjutsu.* When and where these practices originated is obscured by conflicting legends. During the warring Sengoku period, ninja and the use of *ninjutsu* flourished. Many trained in the art of *ninjutsu* were from the Iga region (now Mie Prefecture) and the Koka region of Omi Province (now Shiga Prefecture). These two mountainous areas near Kyoto became hotbeds of ninja activities. Some of the ninja were former samurai and *jizamurai* peasant-warriors, so the majority came from the lower class. This partly accounts for the lack of information on the ninja. The upper-class samurai were noted for writing, and there are many accounts of their exploits, whereas the lower class did almost no writing; moreover, what they did was of little interest to the majority of Japanese.

There is no denying the frequent use of ninja by warlords. Tokugawa Ieyasu relied extensively on them in his campaigns. The ninja were despised by many samurai because these warriors in black clothing were considered outsiders, not part of the retinue serving the lord. With the absence of warfare in the Edo period, the ninja disappeared as a group, and former ninja were employed as security guards by the shogunate, but their legacy continued. *Shinobi* manuals based on Chinese military philosophy were available, and interest in *shinobi* techniques was revived. The image of the ninja entered popular culture in the Edo period and is found in folktales and theater plays. In the Meiji period, a cult following of *shinobi* developed, and the techniques used became popular and referred to as *ninjutsu* or stealth by American writers.

Today, ninja appear in many forms in Japanese and Western popular media and games. They are usually dressed head to foot in black, but in real life, they wore ordinary clothes and blended into the population. They were known for using a disguise but preferred not to stand out. Ninja have become pop culture heroes in books, films, television, video games, anime, and manga. The portrayal of ninja ranges from historically accurate accounts to pure fantasy. An example of fantasy is the novel by Eric Van Lustbader, *The Ninja*, published in 1980. The hero is part-Japanese, born and raised in postwar Japan, who studies *ninjutsu* and becomes a ninja. The action takes place in New York City and Long Island. Not surprisingly, the story is full of gruesome violence and killings using ninja techniques and weapons.[88] In reality, the majority of ninja operations were conducted quietly with disguise and deceptive means, and, if possible, violence was avoided. However, these novels needed a lot of action to engage the reader. Sometimes, fantasy could have eerie replication. The use of drones to drop bombs in the Russia-Ukraine war is similar to the ninja use of kites to drop bombs.

Bansenshukai (Ten Thousand Rivers Flowing Together to Form an Ocean), published in 1676, is an original manual that describes

---

88 Eric Van Lustbader, *The Ninja* (London, Grafton Books, 1980).

the production and practical use of secret devices and weapons.[89] It includes volumes on military strategy, but the sections on tools and weapons are of particular interest and are continually consulted. One weapon mentioned that has become popular is *shuriken,* also known as "throwing stars." The toss object originally came in many different shapes, but the most prominent is a star. *Shuriken* was considered a secret weapon of the ninja but was not a killing weapon. It was meant to slow down attackers or used as a distraction. Today, *shurikens* are used for exercising or playing a game similar to darts. A few of the fanciful equipments of the ninja have come into use, but they are still the exception. In the end, the ninja, for all the hyperbole, were not superhuman with magical powers. They were mere mortal fighters with specialized skills. Their supposed exploits during the era of clan and domain warfare have become part of folklore and legends. It makes for entertaining stories, but their influence on the mythical samurai image was marginal.

---

89 English translation is available in Antony Cummins and Yoshie Minami, trans., *The Book of Ninja: The First Complete Translation of the Bansenshukai* (London: Watkins Publishing, 2013).

CHAPTER FIVE

MODERN SAMURAI

Historians date the beginning of the modern period in Japanese history from the collapse of the Tokugawa and the emergence of the Meiji regime in 1868. The antecedents of the modern era could be traced back to the late Tokugawa. The rise of the castle towns with their bustling economy of trade and entrepreneurship were signs of the new age. Moreover, the level of education had risen, providing the necessary resources to propel advancement.

In regards to the samurai, the antecedents could be pushed back even further to the actions by Hideyoshi, stripping the samurai from their land and placing them in castle towns. This had an enormous impact on the samurai. It affected their economic status, removed their livelihood from the land, and made them dependent on the stipend given by the *daimyo* and shogunate. Samurai found the stipend inadequate and their functional role problematic, leading to financial and emotional stress. Domestic conditions made it ripe for drastic changes to take place.

And dramatic changes did take place with the emergence of the modern samurai. The modern samurai evolved during the mid-nineteenth century and existed for about fifty years. It paralleled the existence of the traditional cowboy, which lasted about forty years.

Therefore, the period of the modern samurai occurred at the same time as the traditional cowboy and lasted for about the same length of time.

DEVELOPMENT AND FOREIGN INFLUENCE

What were the domestic conditions that brought on the modern samurai? Here a brief summary of the conditions is necessary. In 1600, the beginning of the Edo period, the population of Japan was estimated to be somewhere between eighteen and twenty-two million. By 1873, the first decade of the Meiji period, the population was approximately 33.3 million. Using the average figure of twenty million for the population in 1600, this is an increase of 67 percent, a significant rise, mainly in the urban centers. The samurai were concentrated in the towns and cities, and their families comprised about 5 to 6 percent of the population. The number of samurai depends on how the class is defined. As previously noted, at the top were the *daimyo,* and their number had stabilized when the fighting and chaos ended. Immediately below were several grades of samurai that formed their retinue. At the bottom were the *jizamurai,* the part-time soldiers who were peasant farmers. When the land was taken from them, and they did not move into the castle towns, they lost their status as samurai and became full-time farmers, although they could still be recruited as foot soldiers. Those who moved into the castle towns became soldiers, and with the absence of warfare, they were used as guards, messengers, and clerks. The Tokugawa shogunate followed through with their social control by establishing a rigid class structure, lessening the possibility of social mobility. The class structure defined who the samurai were, but there was ambiguity at the lowest level—the *jizamurai* and *ashigaru.* Depending on the historical period, there was shifting in how the lower classes were defined.

Samurai status was visibly and symbolically shown by the possession of weapons. As warriors, swords were the tools of their profession, but the exclusive privilege of being the only ones allowed to have armaments came much later. In 1588, weapons were taken away from the peasants and all others. It is at this juncture that the sword is turned into a status symbol. The implication of this change was that, in the long run, it signaled the the loss of its raison d'être—using the sword to fight and defend against adversaries. Its duties were reduced to serving as a garrison for the *daimyo's* castle, as escort on journeys to and from Edo, and policing the *daimyo's* land. The only serious unrests were peasant revolts, limited to areas of severe economic dislocation. Since the peasants were unarmed, these disturbances were quickly quashed. The sword was not needed for defensive purposes.

Although the taxes imposed on the peasants were onerous and caused many destitute peasants to revolt, a more critical issue for the Tokugawa shogunate was the samurai class. The samurai problem was financial, caused by decreased domain revenues, which resulted in the issuance of insufficient samurai stipends. The stipends were paid in rice, and the amount varied with the samurai's rank and status, the wealth of the domain, and the land productivity. An average samurai received about one hundred *koku* of rice annually but other grains could be used. If gains were substituted, the samurai would suffer a loss since rice had the greatest value. The domains were financially stressed as land productivity had reached its maximum, and no further improvement could be made.

Meanwhile, the population had increased, which meant a rise in demand with limited supply. Expenses were heavy with the maintenance of another residence in Edo and the mandatory journeys to and from Edo. The samurai of distant domains were particularly affected but were also more numerous. Coupled with the financial stress was the poor morale. Employment in urban centers was limited, and most samurai were not trained, skilled, or inclined to seek other means of employment. They remained hopelessly disaffected. Yamaga Soko, the Tokugawa scholar, arrived at a rationale for the existence of the samurai in a time of peace. Samurai were to serve as moral models for society, the embodiment of austerity, self-discipline, duty, trust, and loyalty. Still, the dysfunctional feeling did not go away. Instead, it worsened as the samurai were forced to incur debt, borrowing from the despised merchants, the lowest class in Japanese society. Samurai in the impoverished lower level blamed the well-to-do upper samurai for their predicament—it was a problem of income inequality.

The Tokugawa *bakuhan* system of a centralized military government with outlying domains was designed to maintain the status quo. Its rigid occupational groupings and policies prevented significant changes from taking place. Yet, there comes a time in a country's history when the convergence of socioeconomic and political forces reaches a critical point where alterations must occur. Such a point was reached in mid-nineteenth century Japan. A shock was needed to set it off, and it came from the West.

Europeans first came to the southern islands of Japan in the mid-sixteenth century. They travelled through the Indian Ocean, the Strait of Malacca, and the South China Sea. Their first encounter was with the Portuguese traders. In the ensuing two centuries, the Portuguese were followed by traders from Spain, Holland, and England. These occasional contacts were concentrated around Nagasaki. During this time, Christian missionaries arrived, and their presence was strong in and around the Nagasaki region. Since these foreigners came from the South, they were known as "Southern barbarians."

By the early seventeenth century, Protestant missionaries arrived as rivals to the Catholic priests. Christian missionaries had surprising success, and according to one estimate, more than three hundred thousand Japanese were converted in Kyushu. Included in the conversion were a few *daimyo* and their families, and this was consequential, for it meant their retinue would have to follow suit. How deep their faith was is a matter of conjecture. Samurai officials reacted by enforcing the 1614 edict, expelling missionaries and placing a nationwide ban on Christianity. Christians were forbidden to proselytize Japanese into Christianity. The samurai authorities embarked on a cruel campaign of persecution and punishment. *Kakure Kirishitan* (Hidden Christians) were ferreted out, tortured, burned at the stake, and even crucified. One method used to expose Christians was to have people step on a wooden board with the likeness of Christ or Mary. If they hesitated or refused, they were arrested and tortured. In 1639, the *sakoku* (closed country) policy finally sealed the country, forbidding foreigners from entering Japan and the Japanese from traveling abroad. It was assumed the "closed country" edict had eradicated Christianity from Japan. Amazingly, a small group of Hidden Christians survived, and for seven generations, passed on the religion without Bibles or priests. They successfully hid from the samurai officials and survived, but the result was a perverted form of Christianity. The persecution of Christians resulted in over four thousand dying because of their faith and thousands of others suffering deprivation and ruined lives.[90] The samurai authorities followed the vicious policy for political and ideological reasons. Foreigners were viewed as a subversive threat, and an alien religion, such as Christianity, could undermine loyalty to one's lord and the shogun.

Soon, an event would end the Tokugawa shogunate's *sakoku* policy, which had endured for over two hundred years. On July 8, 1853, four foreign warships appeared off Uraga, a village at the mouth of Edo Bay, now known as Tokyo Bay. People in that area were startled by the sight of these ships, two of which were coal-burning steamships. The Japanese called these vessels "Black Ships" because the hulls were black, and the steam-driven vessels belched black smoke.

Commodore Matthew Calbraith Perry commanded the American expedition. He carried a letter from President Millard Fillmore asking for trade relations. Already, Americans were involved in the Chinese trade, following in the footsteps of the European powers as "unequal treaties" opened Chinese ports to Western commerce. This was simply an extension of America's Asian market. In addition, the US government sought better treatment of shipwrecked sailors and access to ports where whaling ships could replenish their supplies.

The reaction of the samurai leadership was initially one of shock, stress, and annoyance but was soon replaced by curiosity and fascination. What was immediately apparent was the lack of means to expel these foreigners. While the Japanese officials decided what to do, the Americans scouted the bay. Perry came ashore five days later, formally dressed, and marched in with pomp and ceremony. He handed over President Fillmore's letter to the shogunate officials. There was an exchange of gifts, and one gift caught everybody's attention: a miniature steam locomotive that ran on a track and was large enough to hold a child. It displayed the technological prowess of the West.

---

90 John Dougill, *In Search of Japan's Hidden Christians: A Story of Suppression, Secrecy and Survival* (Rutland, VT: Tuttle Publishing, 2012), xi. See also the historical fiction, *Silence,* by novelist Endo Shusaku. It was made into an American movie with the same name in 2016 with Martin Scorsese as director. There is also a Japanese film adaptation of Endo's novel with the same name and was released in 1971. It was directed by Shinoda Masahiro.

Perry's landing ceremony

The Japanese public learned about the American arrival through *kawaraban* (single-sheet woodblock prints). They viewed the *kawaraban* drawings of the ships, the landing ceremony, and the exchange of gifts with interest. Included in the woodblock prints were drawings of the preparations undertaken by individual samurai and the defensive deployment against the black ship.[91] The defensive drawings were to demonstrate the leadership's response to the arrival of the foreigners.

Commodore Perry's visit was relatively short. He left on July 14, five days after arrival at Uraga, but he left a message, saying he would return soon with a larger squadron and awaited the shogunate's response. Perry kept his promise and returned seven months later, on February 13, 1854, with nine vessels, including three steam-driven ships. The fleet anchored near Yokohama and Koshiba. It was an impressive fleet with over one hundred guns and a complement of approximately 1,800 crew members. This time, there were more interactions, including gift exchanges, banquets, and entertainment. A sumo demonstration was performed, and the Americans offered a minstrel show wearing blackface. The main event was the signing of the Treaty of Kanagawa

---

91 John W. Dower, "Black Ships & Samurai: Commodore Perry and the Opening of Japan [1853-1854]" (Cambridge, MA: Visualizing Cultures, Massachusetts Institute of Technology, 2010). visualizingcultures.mit.edu > black_ships…

on March 31, 1854. Almost all of the US government's requests were met. The only exception was the omission of trade rights. The Japanese agreed to treat castaways humanely and to open two ports, Shimoda and Hakodate, to supply provisions and shelter. A major breakthrough was the Japanese government's reluctant acceptance of the American proposal to station a "consul" in Shimoda. Once this happened, Japan was essentially "opened." European powers (British, French, Dutch, and Russian) followed the lead of the Americans and eventually won similar concessions from the Japanese government.

Within the highest circles of policymakers in the Tokugawa government, there was disagreement on handling negotiations with the Americans. The shogunate consulted with the *daimyo,* but they offered conflicting views. One group advocated for rejecting the foreigners' proposals even if it meant war. Others supported a compromising approach to gain time so the country could prepare defensively. The resulting decision to accept the American proposal led to widespread criticism, the harbinger of the movement to replace the Tokugawa regime.

Townsend Harris arrived in August 1856 and became the first American consul at Shimoda. At first, he was not welcomed, and the Japanese made it difficult for him to accomplish anything. His principal task was to obtain a trade treaty with Japan, which was arduous because the Japanese ignored him. Meanwhile, Britain and France, through the use of force, had obtained large concessions from China. Harris was able to use this information, warning the Japanese that it would be catastrophic if a trade treaty were not signed between the US and Japan because Britain was planning to extract onerous concessions. To avoid such a threat, the Japanese officials conceded and both countries signed the Treaty of Amity and Commerce between Japan and the United States (Harris Treaty) on July 29, 1858.

Townsend Harris

In increasingly poor health and concerned about politics in his home state, Harris resigned from his position in 1861 and returned to New York. Japanese officials appreciated his efforts, and he was respected and viewed favorably. His crowning achievement was the Harris Treaty, but he understood the limitations of the Japanese government and was aware of its political problems. Unfortunately for the Tokugawa government, it did not end there, and in the following ten years, the European powers were able to extract similar trade treaties. All of these treaties proved to be constant irritants and embarrassed the shogunate. It added to the arguments for replacing the government and finally in 1868 the Meiji government was established.

In 1958, *The Barbarian and the Geisha*, a film about Townsend Harris, was released. It was directed by John Huston and starred John Wayne. Yes, the cowboy hero played the role of Harris. I imagine it was difficult for American movie viewers to dismiss the image of a rugged cowboy in the role of Harris, a patient diplomat struggling in a Japanese setting. How incongruous—but Wayne gave a commendable performance. Generally speaking, the film follows the true story of Harris' stint as consul. However, the subplot of his love affair with Tojin Okichi is fictitious. She was a real person but worked as a servant for only three months. Some scenes were created for melodramatic effect, and others were just fantasies.

It is with Commodore Perry that the full impact of Western influence was first felt, and this led to the transformation of the traditional samurai myths. However, there were earlier foreigners that changed the thinking of the samurai elite. One such foreigner was William Adams (1564-1620), who has been mythologized to some degree by writings, movies, and television series. In *Shogun,* the novel by James Clavell, the main protagonist is John Blackthorne, who uses the Japanese name Anjin, which means "pilot." Anjin or Blackthorne is based on the historical figure of Adams, an English navigator, so we see how the name Anjin was derived. In the story, Anjin is one of the few survivors of a shipwreck. After being imprisoned, the Japanese realized his value as a source of information, and he becomes an advisor to the *daimyo.* In the novel, various subplots and love interests revolve around Anjin, most of which are fabrications. But his role as a confidant of the *daimyo* is accurate and most important.

In 1600, William Adams became the first Englishman to reach Japan when he survived the wreck of a Dutch trading ship. The shogun, Tokugawa Ieyasu, was eager to learn more about what was happening throughout the world, and Adams provided the much-sought information. Adams persuaded the shogunate to establish a Dutch and English trading post at Hirado, a small island near Nagasaki. Furthermore, he helped in the construction of Western-style ships, trained the Japanese in the use of cannons, and served with the Tokugawa army. For his services, Ieyasu conferred the status of *hatamoto* and gave Adams a mansion with housekeepers, a monthly allowance, and a daily allotment of rice. It is said that Adams became a samurai, but that is not true; he was given an honorary title.

Adams was an advisor to Ieyasu, but there were other foreign advisors, although none were purported to be as influential, and few reached the higher echelon of the Tokugawa shogunate. Foreign advisors became important in the Meiji period, and significant contributions were made at that time in medical science, law, administration, economics, engineering, education, agriculture, and military science. They were known collectively in Japanese as *O-yatoi Gaikokujin* (hired foreigners). All of these foreign influences had a profound impact on the thinking and behavior of the samurai. Some would say the foreign ideas and ways were contradictory and disruptive, while others say they were supplementary and supportive. Regardless, it did lead to the transformation of the mythivcal samurai.

MYTHS AND REALITIES

Myth: Samurai were men of extremes—they were idealists

The samurai class evolved over seven centuries. How it viewed itself depended on the development stage and the conditions of that time. For the early samurai, there were no codes or ideologies but there were idealistic expressions in the "house instructions" (*kakun*) of the samurai clans. The clan instructions were first written during the Kamakura period. They provide insights into how the samurai viewed themselves and their function in society. These moral guidelines were handed down from the clan leaders to the young samurai and were not meant for aristocrats or commoners. During the seventeenth century, *kakun* were even prepared for merchant houses and wealthy farmers. Most of the precepts dealt with practical matters. These documents present different views on the ideals of the warrior. Following are a few *kakun* quotations:

> Learning is to a man as the leaves and branches are for a tree, and can be said that he should simply not be without it. *The Iwamizudera Monogatari.*
>
> Takeda Shingen (1521-1573).

> No matter whether person belongs to the upper or lower ranks, if he has not put his life on the line at least once he has cause for shame. *Lord Nabeshima Wall Inscriptions.*
>
> Nabeshima Naoshige (1538-1618).

> I will stand off the forces of the entire country here...and die a resplendent death.
>
> *The Last Statement of Torii Mototoda* (1539-1600).

> Having been born into the house of a warrior, one's intentions should be to grasp the long and short swords and to die. *The Precepts of Kato Kiyomasa.*
>
> Kato Kiyomasa (1562-1611).[92]

When it came to specific samurai virtues of loyalty, bravery, and honor, they were extolled and highlighted in the heroic stories, especially

---

92 Lee, *Ideals of the Samurai*, 95, 113, 119, 127.

in the later versions of the historical chronicles. The precedent of recounting the valorous samurai was set in *The Tale of the Heike*. In the stirring stories, the virtues of loyalty and bravery were emphasized. The ideals were repeated so often they became ingrained in the thinking of the samurai.

Constant warfare made the ideals of bravery, loyalty, and honor the uppermost concern. However, in the absence of warfare in the Tokugawa period, there was a need to buttress the samurai ideals to prevent them from deteriorating. As a result, advocates of the samurai class began to write about the "way of the samurai," the beginning of what became known as Bushido.

One writer concerned with the role of the samurai in a peacetime environment was a *ronin*, Kumazawa Banzan (1619-1691), a disciple of the Oyomei school.[93] Oyomei believed in the unity of knowledge and action; that is, one must have an understanding but, at the same time, take action. If you know, you must act. Just giving verbal assent is inadequate to demonstrate actual knowledge. Kumazawa's writings later inspired the young leaders of the Meiji Restoration.

Kumazawa personally put into practice what he thought the samurai should do. In his essay "The Model Samurai," he followed a physical training program and dietary regimen to meet the required fitness. He believed a samurai must not only be physically ready but mentally and intellectually as well.[94] His writing was not theoretical; he did what he wrote about. Kumazawa believed that as a samurai, he had to serve as a model for others to follow.

Of all the writers on Bushido, the most influential was Yamaga Soko, often referred to as the "father of Bushido." He was a *ronin* like Kumazawa Banzan and worked hard to establish himself. Yamaga was influenced by Neo-Confucianism, which emphasizes the moral behavior of the samurai. He wrote that the samurai class was not a parasite living at the expense of other social classes. Since the samurai had more freedom, he should cultivate those arts and virtues that would enable him to be a model and leader for society. He wrote in extreme detail about the ideals of the samurai and the qualities the samurai class had long honored—devotion to duty, temperance, austerity, and

93 Oyomei is the Japanese translation of the name Wang Yangming, the sixteenth-century Chinese philosopher who advocated the intuitive approach. This was in opposition to the reason or rational approach of Zhu Xi, the leading Neo-Confucian philosopher.

94 Wm. Theodore de Bary, ed. *Sources of Japanese Tradition* (New York: Columbia University Press, 1958), 387-88.

self-discipline. It was now codified, and in the process, it became more rigid. The myth of the samurai as a moral paragon was solidified, thus widening the gap between the ideal and the reality.

There is another aspect of Yamaga's writings, his study of military science, that is not as well known. It was contrary to his Confucianist training. Although moral training of the samurai was essential, in his view, so was military learning. He stressed the importance of studying and adopting Western weapons and tactics. There was a need to know the enemy and this meant learning more from the West. During the transition phase that the Japanese underwent in the mid-nineteenth century, this seemingly paradoxical stance was the key to the successful transformation of the samurai leadership.

Another writing that helped rationalize the samurai class's existence in a time of peace was the *Hagakure* (*Hidden by the Leaves*), a collection of sayings and anecdotes. These were casual thoughts from an elderly samurai, Yamamoto Tsunetomo (1645-1716). Compiled from 1710 to 1716, it covered a wide range of subjects, but the principal focus was on the distinguishing characteristics of the samurai class. It opens with the famous passage:

> The Way of the Samurai is found in death. When it comes to either/or, there is only the quick choice of death. It is not particularly difficult. Be determined and advance.[95]

The precepts are idealistic and intuitive rather than rational and are based on sincerity. Sincerity, or *makoto*, is a samurai value often used to justify actions toward death. An aphorism on sincerity is as follows:

> Sincerity is the Way of Heaven. To make oneself sincere is the Way of man. He who is sincere hits the mark without effort and grasps the situation without effort and grasps the situation without thinking.[96]

Written when there was no fighting, Yamamoto faced the problem of maintaining the samurai class, and his words reflected his nostalgia for a world that had disappeared. For many years, *Hagakure* was known only by samurai of the Nabeshima clan in what is now Saga prefecture

---

95 Yamamoto Tsunetomo, *The Pocket Hagakure: The Book of the Samurai,* trans. William Scott Wilson (Boulder, CO: Shambhala Publications, 2019), 3.

96 Yamamoto, *The Pocket,* xxviii.

in Kyushu. Later, it became a classic explanation of samurai thought. In modern times, it was used by the Japanese military during World War II. The nationalist writer Mishima Yukio was inspired by *Hagakure* and wrote the following in his book, glorifying self-destruction:

> The occupation of the samurai is death. No matter how peaceful the age, death is the samurai's supreme motivation, and if a samurai should fear or shun death, in that instant he would cease to be a samurai.[97]

While the compilation of the *Hagakure* was taking place, a group of scholars of the Mito school (*Mitogaku*) advocated nativism, isolationism, and reverence of the emperor. These ideas developed from the project compiling the *Dai Nihon-shi* (*A History of Great Japan*). As the Mito school progressed during the nineteenth century, it began to focus on anti-foreign ideology and the importance of the emperor. The slogan "*sonno joi*" ("revere the emperor, expel the barbarians") was adopted by the school. A polemical Mito writing was *Shinron* (*New Proposals*) by Aizawa Seishisai (1782-1863). He was the first to systematically advocate anti-Western ideas and the need to protect Japan from the "barbarians" by promoting nativism and opposing Western arms, trade, and religions. He argued that supporting the emperor was a way to confront the Western threat. According to Aizawa, the Japanese emperor is the direct descendant of the Sun Goddess and serves as a model for other nations to follow. The *New Proposals* later inspired the samurai leaders of the Meiji Restoration.

Morality was important in the Mito school. If morality breaks down or there is a lack of moral leadership, it could lead to the demise of the Japanese civilization. Therefore, the problem could be an internal rather than an external threat. Furthermore, the argument was made that the emperor had given the Tokugawa shogunate the power to handle pressing financial problems, but it failed to act because it lacked moral leadership, and this caused the domains to be financially and militarily weak.

It was at this juncture that Tokugawa Nariaki (1800-1860) became the *daimyo* of Mito in 1829. He was a leading figure in the nationalist movement in the 1850s and 1860s and the most vocal defender of

---

97 Mishima Yukio, *On Hagakure: The Samurai Ethic and Modern Japan.* trans. Kathryn Sparling (Tokyo: Charles E. Tuttle, 1978), 27.

Japan's seclusion policy—the policy to keep out foreigners. A strong supporter of the Mito slogan of *sonno joi,* he criticized the shogunate for its moral decay, the resulting financial instability, and its inability to protect Japan from foreign intrusions. Social reforms were instituted in his domain to maintain the Neo-Confucianist hierarchical social structure. Economic reforms were undertaken to strengthen the domain from shogunate intrusion, peasant rebellion, and foreign attack. Nariaki was adamant on the anti-foreign policy, yet he was open to importing foreign ideas and technology. As long as it could be used to strengthen Mito, it was perfectly acceptable to import foreign contributions. The contradiction was not a concern. Moreover, Nariaki was a descendant, a blood relative of Tokugawa Ieyasu, the founder of the *bakufu.* By advocating "revere the emperor," he undermined his family background and eventually caused the Tokugawa shogunate to collapse. It was another contradiction in his thinking. Nariaki and the Mito school did not intend for the overthrow of the *bakufu,* but their ideas united and inspired the insurgents and led to the Meiji Restoration.

There were further attempts to rationalize the existence of the samurai class in a peacetime environment and to delineate its role clearly. At times, there were disputes when interpreting the values, virtues, and their applications. Nevertheless, these ideals were further solidified in the thinking of the samurai elite and began to permeate throughout Japanese society. Commoners took on samurai ideals as these virtues were popularized by stories of Minamoto no Yoshitsune and other heroes. As we have seen, the story of the Forty-Seven Ronin was presented in several ways, including puppet plays, and was recreated in the kabuki play *Chushingura.* Thus, samurai values spread to all classes in Japanese society. When the samurai class was abolished in the 1870s, the values persisted because the ideals were diffused thoroughly and had become a part of Japanese culture. Although muted to a large degree by Western influence, traditional samurai values still characterize Japanese thinking.

Myth: Samurai were men of extremes—they were pragmatists

Contrary to the myth that the samurai were men of high principles and idealism, they also had a practical side. The samurai were always looking for an advantage or an improvement in the role of modern

Japan. They did not have to wait long because the first break came in the field of military technology.

Among the Japanese samurai, there was always a liking for Western arms. It was by way of China that the Japanese became aware of cannons and the possibilities of their use. The Japanese made copies of the early cannons, but they were heavy, crude, and were seldom used. Then, in 1543, firearms were introduced in Japan by shipwrecked Portuguese seamen on Tanegashima, a small island south of Kyushu. There were matchlock guns, sometimes called arquebus or the Japanese term, *tanegashima,* after the island where they were discovered. It was a cumbersome weapon, but the Japanese were intrigued and understood its potential. The use of firearms spread quickly. At this time the cannons obtained from the Portuguese were implemented. Since they were heavy and immobile, they were used for siege tactics and coastal defense. The matchlocks were more easily adopted. Local *daimyo* recognized the superiority of Western arms and immediately ordered craftsmen to duplicate the Portuguese matchlock. Soon, their craftsmen could replicate and produce them in large quantities. It is surprising how quickly they were able to do this, allowing them to manufacture their version of the weapon and not rely on the importation of arms. This was a key decision.

The next step was to learn how to use firearms in combat. There was sporadic use of matchlocks in Sengoku battles, but plans were made for strategic implementation. In 1549, Oda Nobunaga bought five hundred matchlocks and formed a firearm brigade. Takeda Shingen, the *daimyo* of Kai province (now Yamanashi Prefecture), adopted firearms in the 1550s and began to use them. By the late sixteenth century, matchlocks became the most important offensive weapon. The superiority of firearms was decisively demonstrated in the Battle of Nagashino in 1575. Nobunaga employed more than three thousand musketeers, who were *ashigaru* trained in these new weapons. He divided them into three rows and had them fire their guns in sequence. This gave time for reloading, thus achieving a steady volley of fire. They fired their matchlock muskets while standing behind a temporary fence designed to ward off horses. In the Nagashino battle, Takeda Katsuyori, the successor of Takeda Shingen, led his vaunted cavalry against the temporary fence but was met with a barrage of fire that quickly decimated them. The mounted samurai with swords and spears were no match for the muskets. It ended in a disastrous defeat of the Katsuyori's army, signaling the end of the Ashikaga shogunate and brought on the ascendancy of the Oda and Tokugawa forces.[98]

The final symbolic triumph of Western firearms over samurai swords occurred with the Satsuma Rebellion of 1877, the last resistance of the samurai. In a series of skirmishes in Kyushu, the national conscript army, mostly comprised of commoners equipped with rifles, inflicted mounting casualties and routed the samurai rebels. By the end, the samurai were out of ammunition for their weapons and only had swords. On the morning of September 24, 1877, the remaining forty samurai made their final suicidal charge and were cut down by gunfire on the hill of Shiroyama. There was no bravado with the sword when faced with gunfire. It meant not only the end of the Satsuma Rebellion but the end of the samurai class. The Hollywood version of this battle is depicted in *The Last Samurai* (2003), directed and produced by Edward Zwick and starring Tom Cruise and Ken Watanabe. The film was widely acclaimed in Japan, whereas it did not receive such a response in the US. Japanese appreciated the sympathetic portrayal of the samurai. The myth lives on, and some Japanese mourn what the nation lost in its drive towards modernity.

The use of firearms caused radical changes in the methods of warfare. The mounted samurai was no longer useful. Close combat with swords and spears was replaced by long-range combat and foot soldiers with muskets. The higher-class samurai were replaced by the lower-class peasants armed with guns. Pragmatism had overtaken idealism.

The interest in Western ways was more than military technology. When the *bakufu* instituted the seclusion policy that excluded all Western contacts, they kept a door open at Deshima, allowing a small group of Dutch and Chinese traders to reside on the island. Studies have focused on the Dutch, but the Chinese traders were an important source of information on what was occurring in China. Unequal treaties were imposed on the weak Chinese government by the European powers, and these reports served as valuable intelligence

---

98 The Battle of Nagashino is recounted in the 1980 epic film, *Kagemusha* (Shadow Warrior), directed by Akira Kurosawa. It is based on the daimyo Takeda Shingen and his clan, but the "shadow warrior" is fictitious.

on what could happen to Japan. In addition, the Japanese wanted nonpolitical information on science and technology from the Dutch officials. Research has shown how active *rangaku* (Dutch studies) was in trying to keep abreast with Western scientific knowledge and technology. What started as a trade exchange gradually moved to an exchange of knowledge. The eighth shogun, Tokugawa Yoshimune, allowed the import of non-Christian books and promoted the Dutch language and Western book translations, especially books on medicine and other fields of science. Dutch studies soon extended beyond Deshima to other parts of the country. At times, it became a family pursuit, passing from one generation to another. Later, English and German books became the primary sources of information, but for many years Chinese and Dutch books were the only resources available.

With the arrival of American, British, French, and Russian ships and the pressured signing of treaties with these countries, Japan realized how weak it was defensively and how backwards it was in technology. The Japanese started to study Western science with greater intensity. It began as early as 1855 with the establishment of a naval training center in Nagasaki. The government ordered steam warships from the Dutch but, at the same time, rescinded the ban on building ocean-going boats. It helped to bring about a shipbuilding yard in Nagasaki. Japan was to construct its own ships and not rely on or purchase vessels from other countries. It was the beginning of the Japanese plan to have their own strategically important industrial facilities, including iron foundries and factories to build steam engines.

In 1857, the government started a language training center in Nagasaki where English, French, Russian, Dutch, and Chinese were taught. Language instruction was broadened—*rangaku* (Dutch studies) became *yogaku* (Western studies). Language schools were opened in other cities. In 1860, the shogunate sent the first diplomatic and study mission to the US, and to expand ties with other foreign countries, two more missions were sent to European countries. What took place next, the Iwakura Mission of 1871 to the United States and Europe, was of major importance. The purpose of the mission was to learn about Western advancements, renegotiate unequal treaties, establish diplomatic relations, and determine the best ways to modernize. There were forty-eight mission members, and students were included, bringing the total to about one hundred participants. Three samurai who later became leaders in the Meiji government were members.[99] After extended visits to the US and the United Kingdom, the tour made short trips to a few other European countries before returning home in 1873. The mission took almost two years.

What is significant in these activities is a small group of samurai were at the forefront, promoting Western knowledge and technology. It seemed contradictory for these samurai to seek Western knowledge while strongly holding on to traditional ideals. But the samurai believed traditional values could exist side-by-side with Western learning— they could be symbiotic. A samurai scholar and writer from Shinano province, Sakuma Shozan (1811-1864), is noted for the slogan he made famous, "Eastern ethics and Western science" ("*Toyo no dotoku, Seiyo no gakugei*"). In this slogan, Sakuma summarized his belief that Japanese values (Confucian virtues) are compatible with Western knowledge. He dismissed the inherent contradictions between the two and instead focused on the need to develop military power to prevent the domination of the West and, at the same time, preserve the unity that comes from upholding the traditions of the country. What is noteworthy is how the samurai leaders minimized the contradictions and conflicts that arose when Japanese virtues were paired with Western knowledge. It did not disrupt Japan's march toward modernization.[100]

---

99 The three who became prominent figures in the Meiji government were Ito Hirobumi, Okubo Toshimichi, and Kido Takayoshi.

100 de Bary, *Sources,* 607.

Sakuma Shozan

For those samurai who were not involved in Dutch studies or implementing Western technology, the Western model was important for a different reason. They were motivated by a high level of nationalistic spirit and believed the Western example would not only help defend the country but unify it by restoring sovereign power to the emperor. Western influence, whether rejected or accepted, would be used to restore the emperor's power. Thus, *sonno joi* became the battle cry of the activists seeking the overthrow of the shogunate.

One of the pro-imperial activists was Sakamoto Ryoma (1836-1867). He was a lower-class samurai, a *goshi* (countryside warrior), whose family did not reside in the castle town but in a small village with a farm. This exception to the policy of removing the samurai from the land was only allowed in a few places and far away from Edo, the capital. Besides being a lowly *goshi*, Sakamoto came from Tosa, a minor domain on the island of Shikoku, so he did not have much status.

Sakamoto Ryoma

At an early age, Sakamoto developed into an excellent swordsman. He caught the attention of the *daimyo* and was appointed to join the Tosa delegation in Edo. After his tour, he returned to Tosa and established the local loyalist party, which was only interested in reforming the local government. However, Sakamoto believed that reform was needed for all of Japan. Disenchanted, he left Tosa without authorization in 1862 and became a *ronin*. His initial act at the national level was to assassinate Katsu Kaishu, a high-ranking Tokugawa official involved in the program to modernize the Japanese navy. Katsu was a target of the loyalists because he supported innovation and westernization—both, at that time, were thought by some samurai to be antithetical to restoring power to the emperor. But this thinking changed when the need for rapid modernization became apparent. Katsu persuaded Sakamoto that his long-range program would increase Japan's military strength and deter Western powers. Instead of killing Katsu, Sakamoto decided to become his assistant.

When the shogunate started persecuting loyalists, Sakamoto moved to Kagoshima in the Satsuma domain, a key center of the anti-*bakufu* movement. Here, he took part in negotiating the Satcho Alliance of

1866, a significant development in bringing together the two powerful domains of Satsuma and Choshu in opposition to the Tokugawa. At this time, he formed a trading company in Nagasaki to transport military and assorted supplies to Choshu, Satsuma, and other places. Sakamoto was called back to Tosa to help with the negotiation between the shogun and the emperor. He became the target of anti-loyalist groups, and an assassination attempt was made in March 1866. But Sakamoto was able to fight off the attackers using an American firearm, a Smith and Wesson revolver. Almost two years later, in December 1867, assailants caught up with him in Kyoto, and he was assassinated at age thirty-one.

In his 1867 essay "Eight Proposals While Shipboard," Sakamoto advocated democratic principles such as an elected legislature and a written constitution. Japan would need a national conscript army and navy, and economic reforms would have to be instituted so Japan could compete with Western industry and technology. He was an admirer of Western models and methods to strengthen Japan. But at the same time he was a firm believer and follower of the traditional samurai virtues of loyalty and duty. It was again a combination of pragmatism and idealism.

Sakamoto Ryoma became a national hero. Similar to Kusunoki Masahige, his tragic death magnified his status. This recognition as a hero is a postwar phenomenon. Marius Jansen, a historian of modern Japan, states that Sakamoto was relatively unknown to most Japanese when he began researching on Sakamoto in the 1950s. During this period, the actions and behaviors of the Meiji Restoration forerunners and Meiji government leaders were considered a leading cause for the militarism and nationalistic drive that led to World War II and its disastrous consequences. Japanese people were not ready to honor such leaders. If anything, Sakamoto could be considered a rebel rather than a hero. He had deserted his family and abandoned his loyalty to his feudal lord.

What happened to make Sakamoto one of the most popular heroes? First, the perspective changed. Antipathy towards prewar Japanese leaders had diminished, and Japan had fully recovered from the war. Democratic and peaceful order had taken hold, and there was now an interest in the "rebels" who challenged the old established government. Second, studies were published providing more in-depth information on Sakamoto. The book that made the general public aware of him was the historical novel *Ryoma ga yuku* (*Ryoma Goes His Way*, 1966) by Shiba Ryotaro. The bestseller was based on the true story of Sakamoto. It gave a glowing account of his life.

However, the most significant impetus to the spread of Sakamoto's fame came from the cinema. It took place in the golden age of Japanese cinema when the popularity of *jidaigeki* (historical drama) was at its height. In *Hotarubi* (*Firefly Light*, 1958), the focus was on the first assassination attempt that failed. Shinoda Masahiro's *Ansatsu* (*Assassination*, 1964) came next and was followed by *Bakumatsu* (*End of Tokugawa*, 1970), directed by Ito Daisuke. The films depicted Sakamoto as a revolutionary, but at the same time, an admirer of Western technology and democratic principles. They were romanticized and more violent versions of his life, catering to the prurient interests of the public. A well-known film was Kuroki Kazuo's *Ryoma ansatsu* (*Assassination of Ryoma*, 1974). It reconstructed the last three days of his life. These films depicted Sakamoto as a relatable figure with numerous faults and a complex personality. He was always on the run, trying to avoid his assassins. Because he was the rebels' leader, the shogunate and its allies made him a prime target. It was a departure from the usual image of a traditional, heroic samurai—he was now a hunted victim. The image of the hero had changed; even an evasive rebel could be a hero.

Television took over as the prime platform for spreading the image of Sakamoto. His life story was expanded and presented in a series of television dramas. The highly acclaimed taiga drama, *Ryomaden* (*The Legend of Ryoma*) was shown from January to November 2010. It was a series of forty-eight episodes, had a huge viewership, and greatly impacted Japan. Tourists flocked to Sakamoto's birthplace, museums in Kochi, and the site of his shipping business in Nagasaki. The sale of publications on the television series spiked after the broadcasts.

The younger generation related to Sakamoto's youth, effervescent spirit, and courage. His optimism and ability to quickly accept new ideas were captivating. One of the rare photographs of Sakamoto shows him wearing traditional samurai clothes with Western boots. He carried a cowboy pistol, which saved his life, along with his two samurai swords. Sakamoto had no problem moving from traditional to modern, from Japanese to Western customs. He emerged as a national hero of postwar Japan because of his attractive personality and natural abilities.

Sakamoto was a man with many contradictions. He could support *sonno joi* and fervently uphold the imperial institution, while advocating Western science, technology, and lifestyle. The old, mythical samurai molded to follow only the Japanese pattern was rendered obsolete, and the new leaders were men with contradictions, blending the traditional Japanese ways with Western innovations.

In line with the new image of the mythical samurai presented by Sakamoto, Rurouni Kenshin emerged, a fictional hero who first appeared in a manga series written and illustrated by Nobuhiro Watsuki. It was serialized from April 1994 to September 1999. Two years after the first installment, it was adapted into an anime television series and aired from January 1996 to September 1998. A new anime program was shown in 2023 and will be followed in 2024 by another series. The storyline is based on factual background. It occurred during the Bakumatsu period (the final years of the Tokugawa shogunate) and the early Meiji era. The fictional Kenshin is a wandering *ronin* like Sakamoto. Kenshin was previously an assassin, but he forsook his past and vowed never again to take a life. He tries to find his way in life, and one way is to protect the people with his swordsmanship skills. This is the metamorphosis of Ryoma Sakamoto.

The now-famous *Rurouni Kenshin* is often cited as the most successful samurai anime. It underscores that the historical samurai is still one of the biggest sources of inspiration for Japanese artists. Animators brought samurai history to life by creating stunning fight sequences and serious discussions of honor, loyalty, and friendship. There is a contradiction in maintaining Japanese tradition while assimilating Western ways. In the anime, much imagination and fiction is involved, yet it has bits of historical realism and provides a better understanding of the samurai and his culture.

The fictional accounts showed an evolution in the image of the samurai. In real life, there was a dramatic change in the attitude and behavior of leaders. This shift can be seen with the updated slogans. *Sonno joi* was replaced by *fukoku kyohei* (rich country, strong military). *Sonno joi* was reactionary, overthrowing the Tokugawa shogunate and reestablishing sovereign power to the emperor. Once the rebels attained power, the emperor was made the symbolic head of state. Except for brief periods in Japanese history, emperors did not exercise real political power. The country was ruled by elite families or clans and by the head of the military establishment. Nevertheless, the imperial institution was needed to legitimize rule. With the emperor restored to his rightful position, new leaders could turn from their idealistic posture to more progressive roles—they became pragmatists. They realized Japan had to become a modern state; otherwise, it could not compete and would soon be subjugated by the Western powers. For Japan to be modernized, it would have to follow the pattern of the powerful Western countries—a rich industrial nation with a strong military. Therefore, to be successful in the new world meant having wealth and power, or to put it in Japanese parlance, *fukoku kyohei* or "rich county, strong military."

The new leaders quickly made practical moves. They abolished their dysfunctional samurai class and replaced it with a conscript armed force. Industries, especially those involved with defense, were supported by the government. The ban on building ocean-going ships was dropped, and the government promoted shipbuilding. Railroads, telegraph, and other Western innovations were copied, and soon the Japanese were manufacturing their own versions with the help of foreign advisors.

Westernization meant more than industrialization. There were cultural and political changes. Samurai leaders began to wear Western attire. They read a wide range of books, listened to Western music, and even engaged in Western dancing. Such cultural influence was subsumed under the slogan *bunmei kaika* (civilization and enlightenment). It went beyond customs and fashions; it dealt with Western values. The most prominent exponent of Western knowledge during the Meiji period was Fukuzawa Yukichi (1833-1901). He was an educator, writer, and the founder of Keio University and the newspaper *Jiji Shimpo*. Fukuzawa studied Dutch and English and traveled to America and Europe, so he had personal knowledge of Western civilization. Through his writings and his university and newspaper, Fukuzawa was able to disseminate his views. He wrote the following about the importance of values:

> The strength and progress of the great Western nations…rested on science; and scientific accomplishment, in turn, require a spirit of free inquiry among the general populace. Thus, it followed that liberal and progressive values were not simply moral and political ideals; they were also part and parcel of creating a "rich country, strong military" capable of assuring national independence.[101]

According to Fukuzawa, the task of the nation was to inculcate science and the spirit of independence into the people's thinking so that Japan would grow in wealth and power, rival the West, and be secure from any attack. Traditional Japanese values and ideas were wrong and had to be replaced with Western values and ideology.

Fukuzawa Yuichi

---

101 Walter Donway, "Fukuzawa Yukichi: The Man Who Was 'Civilization and Enlightenment' in Japan." The Reading Room. December 8, 2022. oll.libertyfund.org > reading-room > 202…

Fukuzawa could make such statements because he never entered public service. He was always an outsider and made sweeping suggestions since he was not part of the leadership circle. However, several samurai who made the transition from activists and critical observers to participants in Meiji politics and became high-ranking bureaucrats and policymakers, could not and would not make such compelling recommendations.

In Chapter Four, two prominent statues in Tokyo, Kusunoki Masahige and Saigo Takamori, were cited as examples of samurai who have transitioned into national heroes. There is an imposing statue of Omura Masajiro (1824-1869) in Tokyo's Yasukuni Shrine that isn't as well-known. He is not on the level of Kusunoki and Saigo when it comes to national recognition. Nevertheless, he was an influential Meiji leader, considered the "father of the Japanese army," and played an important role in the modernization of Japan.

Statue of Omura Masajiro, Yasukuni Shrine

Omura was from Choshu, a leading domain in the Meiji Restoration movement. At an early age, he was involved with Dutch studies and worked under the German physician and botanist Philipp Franz von Siebold. Later, he learned English from the American missionary

James Curtis Hepburn. Although from a non-samurai family, he was awarded the samurai status because of his expertise in Western studies. In the 1850s, he became interested in Western military tactics. By the 1860s, he was back in Choshu, teaching at a military academy and helping to reform the domain's army. At this time, he introduced the concept of a modernized army composed of samurai and commoners. It was controversial, but he won his argument in 1866 when his troops defeated the all-samurai force sent to punish the Choshu rebels. Troops organized by Omura became the core of the Satsuma and Choshu armies, which went on to defeat the shogunate forces and led to the overthrow of the Tokugawa government.

In the Meiji government, Omura held a high position and was in charge of creating a national army. He introduced universal military conscription and supported the abolition of the domain system with its private troops. His ideas on modernizing and reforming the military were considered too radical by conservative samurai. It would affect thousands of samurai's lives and end their privileged status. A group of dissident samurai attacked Omura and two associates while they were having dinner, and he was critically wounded. He later died from his wounds.

Although Omura was a believer and promoter of Western methods and advocated abolishing the samurai class, he still upheld the samurai ideals of loyalty and duty. His statue at Yasukuni Shrine shows the dual nature of his personality. He is wearing a *haori* coat and short *hakama* (conventional clothes) and is armed with two swords, all representing the traditional. In his left hand is a binocular, symbolizing the modern. Omura, in many ways, characterized the ex-samurai Meiji leaders. A further look at others, each with a distinctive line of interest, will help to delineate the basic qualities of this small group of elite leaders. There were three, the so-called "Big Three of the Meiji Era." They were: Yamagata Aritomo, who identified with the Japanese imperial army; Okuma Shigenobu (1838-1922) with party politics; and Ito Hirobumi (1841-1909) with constitutional issues.

Yamagata from Choshu was a traditionalist and a nationalist with an interest in the military. In his youth, he traveled abroad and studied the military organization of the Western powers. He was a follower of Omura and carried out several of his proposals. Although Omura had recommended universal military conscription, it was Yamagata who helped to implement it in 1872. He turned the national conscript army into an efficient force. Trained commoners replaced the samurai, and the samurai lost its sole prerogative of being the nation's fighters. The warrior spirit of the samurai was no longer a match for modern arms. In 1882, the *Imperial Rescript to Soldiers and Sailors* was issued to bring the peasants to the samurai level. Like many Meiji documents, several drafts were worked on by a group of officials, but the principal writer was Inoue Kowashi, a compatriot of Yamagata and fellow Meiji oligarch. Since it dealt with the military, Yamagata made some contributions and he had the final say. The following are the *Imperial Rescript* precepts with the ending exhortation:

- consider loyalty an essential duty and do not meddle in politics
- respect superiors and show consideration to those below
- exercise self-discipline and esteem valor
- value faithfulness and righteousness
- aim at simplicity and frugality

> If you, Soldiers and Sailors, in obedience to Our instruction, will observe and practice these principles and fulfill your duty of grateful service to the country, it will be a source of joy, not to Ourself alone, but to all the people of Japan.[102]

---

102 de Bary, *Sources,* 707-08.

Yamagata Aritomo

Yamagata insisted on the separation of the military from politics. He wanted to prevent or forestall the possibility of subversion by political movements. The military was not to be used by any political groups. It had only one loyalty—an unconditional loyalty to the emperor. When the young officers rebelled in the 1930s, they did it not for the sake of politics but for the higher cause of allegiance to the emperor. All of the precepts were undergirded by sincerity. The ethical precepts were Confucian in character and had guided the samurai but now they were applied to the military. It became the official code of ethics for military personnel, and all were required to memorize the *Rescript*.[103]

Yamagata was an astute politician, serving twice as prime minister and in other high Meiji government positions related to national defense. He also served as commander-in-chief of the national conscript army, which suppressed samurai protests and eventually crushed the Satsuma Rebellion in 1877. As previously described in Chapter Four, while washing the severed head of Saigo Takemori, the leader of the rebel army, Yamagata sheds tears over his former colleague. The story captures the essence of Yamagata's character, a true progressive but an idealist at heart.

---

103 Gluck, *Japan's Modern*, 53-54.

A different approach to modernization was taken by Okuma Shigenobu from Hizen, a small domain in Kyushu. He was from a samurai family, and being near Nagasaki, he learned Dutch and English, and was knowledgeable about Western institutions and practices, especially financial subjects and foreign affairs. In 1881, while holding a high position in the government, Okuma called for establishing a constitutional representative government. He was immediately criticized and dismissed from his position. Consequently, Okuma became the principal opposition leader, but even in this supposedly limited status, he achieved gradual political reforms. Within this heated political environment, he balanced the quest for innovations with the need for national unity.

Okuma Shigenobu

Forced out of the government, Okuma became the champion of the political party movement. He founded the Constitutional Progressive Party (*Rikken Kaishinto*), otherwise known as *Kaishinto,* in 1882. The *Kaishinto* called for parliamentary democracy with a constitutional monarchy along the lines of the British model. Once the national Diet was established, he worked with the political parties on reforms. He appealed to a wider segment of the Japanese public and emerged as an advocate of representative democracy. His influence was such that his proteges played major roles in the heyday of party politics in the 1920s.

Okuma diverted his energies to other endeavors and moved Japan into the modern world. He founded Waseda University to prepare students for occupations beyond the government. Waseda was noted for producing prominent journalists, its connections with big business, and its focus on international affairs. In all these diverse interests, his feeling of nationalism remained strong. But at the same time, his love for Japanese traditions did not lessen his acceptance of Western traditions. He drew strength from both traditions as evident in the following statement:

> ...the Japanese are not a race of people who, inconstant and capricious, are given to loving all that is new and curious, always running after passing fashions. They have welcomed Occidental civilization while preserving their old Oriental civilization. They have attached great importance to *bushido,* and at the same time held in the highest respect the spirit of charity and humanity. They have even made a point of choosing the middle course in everything, and have aimed at being always well balanced. To keep exclusively in one direction, or to run to extremes, or to look forward only without looking backward, or to remember one side of a thing, forgetting the other, is not a characteristic of our people. We are conservative simultaneously with being progressive; we are aristocratic and at the same time democratic; we are individualistic while being also socialistic. In these respects we may be said to somewhat resemble the Anglo-Saxon race.[104]

The third Meiji leader under discussion is Ito Hirobumi. He was from dominant Choshu, but his family was from the lowest level of the samurai class. Ito's ability to rise to the highest political status and to become part of the aristocratic society was a hallmark of the early Meiji era, as upward mobility was impossible during previous periods

---

104   Okuma Shigenobu, *Fifty Years of New Japan.* 1st ed., vol. II (London: Smith, Elder, 1909-10), 571-72. Also cited in de Bary, 699-700.

of Japanese history. From early on, Ito studied English and gained firsthand knowledge of the West by traveling abroad. He made a short unauthorized trip to England. At that time, there was still a ban on travel to foreign countries. In 1871, he was part of the Iwakura Mission to the United States and Europe.

Ito Hirobumi

Foremost in Ito's contributions was the establishment of the Meiji Constitution. He had studied German constitutional law and favored the German (Prussian) style constitutional monarchy, although there were a few borrowings from the British model. With the opening of the first parliament, Ito became involved in parliamentary politics. He was the first prime minister and helped form the Friends of Constitutional Government (*Rikken Seiyukai*) party. It was the most powerful political party in the lower house of the Diet from 1900 to 1921. Although known as the "father of the Meiji Constitution" and for his role in establishing parliamentary government, his accomplishments have been dismissed by many Japanese scholars. Ito shifted sides depending on the trends of the time. He moved from one group to another, trying to please everyone. To avoid an impasse, he did not make firm policy decisions in advance, thus leading to indecisiveness. Even leading politicians accused him of opportunism and a lack of principles. The Japanese public respected Ito and recognized his contributions, but scholars and leading politicians scorned him, and historians had difficulty judging him. However, recent studies have led to a reconsideration of the criticisms. Research has shown that Ito had high principles and long-range vision. The give-and-take of politics was necessary to achieve goals—he was, after all, a pragmatic statesman.[105] Ito's idea of a constitutional state was clear (although critics may disagree with its substance), and he worked to achieve it. But Ito did not see its fulfillment; a Korean activist assassinated him during a visit to Harbin, Manchuria.

In an 1899 speech, Ito emphasized the importance of the Western constitutional government for a modern Japan and that the government depends on the responsible exercise of the rights that are given to the people. For the government to work properly, it is the duty of the people to know Japan's history and national polity.

> In this connection what all Japanese must bear in mind is Japan's national polity (*kokutai*). It is history which defines the national polity; thus the Japanese people have a duty to know their history…The national polity of the various countries differs one from another, but it is the testimony of the history of Japan to this day that the unification of the country was achieved around the Imperial House. So I say that the understanding of the national polity of Japan is the first important duty of our people.[106]

---

105   Kazuhiro Takii, Ito Hirobumi - *Japan's First Prime Minister and Father of the Meiji Constitution*, trans. Takechi Manabu (New York: Routledge, 2014), 2-6.
106   de Bary, *Sources*, 677.

The majority of Meiji leaders had firsthand knowledge of Western institutions and practices. They agreed that rapid modernization was needed based on the foreign model. It would enable Japan to compete with other countries. However, with the Western concepts, the Meiji leadership held on to traditional ideals called national polity (*kokutai*). Rapid changes brought fierce arguments on policies and the actions taken, but the social and political fabric of society was not torn asunder by these differences. They were held together by adherence to the traditional ideology. What was seemingly contradictory turned out to be symbiotic. Therefore, the Meiji samurai leaders were pragmatists who were held together by idealistic concepts. They were thoroughly influenced by Western methods and technology and followed the model of the West, yet held on to traditional principals and values. The mythical samurai represented a class that had ruled Japan for about seven centuries and had enormous political, social, and economic impact. Now it was transformed into a mythical figure that was highly educated and achievement-oriented with strong ethics. It was equipped to provide the impetus for the rapid modernization of Japan.

EPILOGUE

Myths are a double-edged sword and could have positive or negative purposes. The positive purposes would include the unification of the country, enhancement of national identity, and the promotion of patriotism and pride in the country's traditions and culture. Heroes are exalted and serve as moral and behavioral models. They exemplify certain virtues to be followed—for the cowboys it would include self-reliance, individualism, courage, steadfastness, trustworthiness, and morally doing the right thing in thought and behavior. For the samurai, it would be their role as warriors and to follow the virtuous line of sincerity, loyalty, duty, courage, self-control, and frugality.

However, myths could be distorted, exaggerated to extremes, and used to legitimized nefarious activities. They can be glorified and made exceptional, so the nation's culture, traditions, and ways of thinking would be superior to those of other countries. It could lead to exceptionalism, the belief that one's country is unique and stands out. When a nation's ideals and practices are considered superior, even if these high principles are carried out with supposedly good intentions, they are bound to provoke criticism and resistance. The tough-minded cowboy approach assumes America has a destined role in the world and other countries should follow in line with American leadership, but other countries view this as arrogant. This cowboy mentality, when applied to US foreign policy, creates controversy and has a polarizing effect.

In prewar Japan, the samurai myth was used to support and promote Japanese expansionism in Korea, Manchuria, China, and Southeast Asia, eventually leading to the Pacific War. A commonly used phrase at that time was *Yamato-damashii* ("Japanese spirit" or "Japanese soul"). Yamato means "Old Japan," where the country originated. The phrase is used today in nationalistic writings, discussions of national character, and the sports media. What *Yamato-damashii* does is heighten the Japanese people and their culture, giving the impression of superiority. It is easy to embed the samurai spirit into the phrase and use it for nefarious purposes.

Another damaging effect of myths is their development as stereotypes. Stereotypes color how people are viewed, and the way their culture and customs are understood. Certain features are characterized and exaggerated, sometimes in a negative way. Americans are seen as having the "cowboy spirit," the values and lifestyles associated with the cowboy, such as rugged individualism, self-confidence, and love of the outdoors, which could also be perceived as arrogance. By contrast, the samurai was pictured as a killing automaton who was stoic and disciplined, and the Japanese people came to be characterized as impassive and orderly.

During the Spanish-American War, Theodore Roosevelt organized the Rough Riders, a thousand-man volunteer group to fight the Spaniards in Cuba. The "cowboy spirit" permeated the group. Roosevelt acted like a cowboy hero when he led the charge up San Juan Hill on his horse, Texas, while the Rough Riders attacked on foot. He became a war hero, and his newly-gained national celebrity enabled him to become president three years later. The "cowboy spirit" colored his foreign policy stance, which was called the "big stick policy," based on the aphorism: "Speak softly and carry a big stick; you will go far." The American press began to use the term "cowboy diplomacy" around 1902 to describe Roosevelt's foreign policies. It is still used today by critics to address the practices of the Ronald Reagan, George W. Bush, and Donald Trump administrations. The term describes how international conflicts are resolved through aggressive risk-taking, bullying, and military deployment. There is a tendency to have an overly simplified, black-and-white worldview and an attempt to remake the world along the lines of American ideals, even if it means doing it alone. Therefore, policies tend to be unilateralist and moralistic. Although, in recent years, there has been a fallback from the hard-liner and ideologically-inclined position to that of a more realistic approach, the tough-minded stance with the "cowboy spirit" remains vibrant. It has waxed and waned, depending on who is in the White House.

In the postwar era of the 1950s, when the US government and businesses played a dominant role in many countries, foreigners came into direct contact with Americans, which gave them a negative impression of Americans as arrogant and ignorant of other cultures. The "ugly American" image tarnished foreign relations for many years. Whether on the diplomatic and business levels or overall policy, the hard-line cowboy attitude and view have affected America's relations abroad.

The cowboy image is highlighted in a film that is a political satire of the Cold War, *Dr. Strangelove* (1964), produced and directed by Stanley Kubrick. The story concerns an unstable US Air Force general who orders a preemptive nuclear attack on the Soviet Union. Attempts were made to recall the B-52 bombers, but one bomber piloted by Major T. J. "King" Kong could not be recalled and continued the mission. A blast from a Soviet defense missile damages the bomb bay doors, so Kong goes back to the bomb bay and does repair work. He is successful, and in the last scene, the bomb bay opens, and the hydrogen bomb drops with Kong straddling it, like a bucking bronco. He rides the H-bomb to the target, wildly waving his Stetson hat and probably yelling "yippee ki-yay."[107]

Some say the last scene is the most memorable in cinematic history. Kubrick wanted a cowboy image, and he needed it to be authentic. John Wayne was offered the role but never responded, so Slim Pickens, a character actor of many Western films, was chosen. Pickens arrived on the set wearing a cowboy hat, boots, and a fringed jacket. His temperament, Texas accent, and behavior showed he was playing it "straight," a real cowboy. Pickens perfectly fitted the role, and "King" Kong exemplified the American free spirit, the "cowboy spirit."

In present-day America, the cowboy myth is evident in the nostalgia for the "good old days" when things were great. According to

---

107 The origin of "yippee ki-yay" is obscure. It is an expression of joy that was widely used by cowboys at least to the nineteenth century. It does not have any particular meaning but is a sound like yodeling found in cowboy songs. Perhaps, it is similar to the Japanese "banzai."

this line of thinking (exceptionalism), American culture is unique and superior, but its "greatness" has been diminished because of corrupting factors. There is a need to return to the ideal state. This is the basis for the watchword "Make America Great Again" (MAGA). It is a nativist political movement that became prominent in the US during the 2016 presidential campaign of Donald Trump. The slogan was first used by Ronald Reagan in the 1980 presidential campaign "Let's Make America Great Again." MAGA assumes there was a "great" nation, but it had lost its luster due to foreign influences through immigration and multiculturalism. Furthermore, globalization is a detriment because it integrates national resources and corrupts the American economy. Diversity, equality, and integration are harmful, and there must have been a time when such influences did not play a major role in American society. However, MAGA does not define when such an ideal condition existed. Historians have shown in their research that any purported ideal period had many ignored or overlooked faults. So-called "good old days" simply did not exist.

MAGA advocates believe America can return to the ideal state through "America first" policies: protecting the economy through tariffs, reducing immigration, especially from third-world countries, and enforcing traditional American values, which are similar to cowboy values. In international relations, America should not be taken advantage of—gross trade imbalances must be corrected, and the US should not carry the heaviest financial burden in alliances and joint projects. The MAGA approach is transactional and nationalistic, reminiscent of the simplistic, tough-minded cowboy approach. Regarding domestic policies, MAGA believes government regulations on the environment, public health, and economic activities should be limited, if not eliminated. It harkens back to the cowboy's ideal of being free and doing things without encumbrance. "Don't fence me in" could be a favorite refrain. MAGA is a broad slogan and vague enough to appeal to those who see it as a patriotic expression of American optimism, the feeling that better times are around the corner. At the same time, it allows for bitter sentiments about the present conditions and for actions to be taken against foreign influence, intrusion, and left-wing elements in American society.

Samurai myths play a conflicting role in present-day Japan, and it is somewhat similar to what has occurred with the cowboy myths—how do you treat the unique traditional ideals and virtues? Bruce Feiler, an American writer, spent a year teaching English in Japan and learned about the myth of Japan's cultural uniqueness. He writes: "This issue of uniqueness has become the number one cultural dilemma facing Japan today. Some argue that the country should overthrow its legacy of isolation and speed up its integration into the rest of the world, while others believe Japan should resist the influx of Western values and stress its own distinctive heritage."[108] The battleground for Feiler was the school classrooms and the minds of the young students.

Japan's Meiji political and military leaders anticipated such a cultural dilemma and took action to avoid or mitigate the consequences as Japan developed into a modern and powerful country. The British historian Oleg Benesch uses the concept of "invented tradition," coined by Eric Hobsbawm, to show how traditional rules, values, and norms of behavior can be transformed and implemented for new purposes.[109] "Invented traditions" were steps taken by nations formed at the end of the nineteenth century to create a nationalistic spirit. It was accomplished by remaking the past. This use of the past to build national unity is a contemporary development. In his extensive research, Benesch explained how the Japanese leaders from Meiji up to World War II utilized modern Bushido, a transformed Bushido, to promote nationalistic fervor. Bushido became an ideology, a helpful tool, for advancing nationalistic pride.[110] However, the rules and values emanating from Bushido are part of the myth of the samurai. Therefore, the samurai myth has also undergone change. It has become a part of Japanese national character.

Another example of the Meiji elite's "invented tradition" was the cult of emperor worship. It culminated with the establishment of State Shinto, wherein Shinto religious practices were incorporated into the national ideology. The government subsidized it, and the belief in the emperor as a divine being was used to inspire national integration, unity, loyalty, and patriotism. Basil Hall Chamberlain (1850-1935),

---

108 Bruce S. Feiler. *Learning to Bow: Inside the Heart of Japan* (New York: Perennial, 2004), 13.
109 Eric Hobsbawm and Terence Ranger, eds., *The Invention of Tradition* (Cambridge, UK: Cambridge University Press, 1983), 1-2.
110 Oleg Benesch. *Inventing the Way of the Samurai: Nationalism, Internationalism, and Bushido in Modern Japan* (New York: Oxford University Press, 2014), 5-7.

an early Japanologist, discerned this new religious invention and wrote about it in his essay *The Invention of a New Religion* (1912).[111] Shinto, which was in decline, was reinvented and used to buttress the imperial institution. The military utilized the newly infused ideology to legitimize its actions by saying it was fighting for the sake of the emperor. Emperor worship was propagated throughout the country. I remember, as a fourth grader in a Japanese language school in Honolulu, there was a portrait of Emperor Hirohito at the front of the classroom, and this was before the Pearl Harbor attack. In Honolulu and other Japanese communities, the emperor's birthday (*Tenchosetsu*) was annually celebrated.[112] All of this was new, taking something from the past and infusing it with new ideas. In the past, emperors were not always exalted; some were embroiled in succession intrigues, some were deposed or exiled, and even assassinated.[113] They were now deified, and the final step of the emperor's divinity was enshrined in the Meiji Constitution. Indoctrination worked, and the Japanese people became firm believers in the myths—even those who formulated the myths believed in their own creation.

There is another analytical construct that is similar to Hobsbawm's "invented traditions." It is what historians refer to as "mythistory." In this concept, myths are as important as history, and both are continually revised. Writers, public officials, and other initiators revive the stories or tales from the past and then rearrange or modify them to explain the present in a new way. Newly created myths could be regularly extended to meet future needs.[114] These amended myths are largely disseminated by the mass media.

Using the concept of mythistory, Carol Gluck, historian of modern Japan, summarizes the Meiji leaders' policies advancing the modernization of the country while at the same time preserving their dominant position by maintaining social stability. Modernization, especially of the military, would help defend against foreign intervention,

---

111 Basil Hall Chamberlain, *The Invention of a New Religion*. Project Gutenberg eBook. Originally published in 1912. www.gutenberg.org > files.

112 It was renamed *Tenno Tanjobi* in 1948 to eliminate the Chinese origin of the term and its association with State Shinto.

113 Takashi Fujitani, *Splendid Monarchy and Pageantry in Modern Japan* (Berkeley: University of California Press, 1998), 2-3.

114 Carol Gluck and Stephen R. Graubard, eds. *Showa: The Japan of Hirohito* (New York: W. W, Norton & Company, 1992), 1-2. The term is from William H. McNeill, *Mythistory and Other Essays* (Chicago: University of Chicago Press, 1986).

but just as critical was the need for "inner spiritual revival" to protect against the excesses of Japanese imbued with Western ways and thoughts, such as materialism and personal success (individualism). The Meiji leadership was concerned about its citizens adopting foreign ideas. The internal threat was as important as the external threat. This is similar to the American nationalists' fear of the influx of immigrants with their values and ideas that could pollute and undermine the American way. Meiji pronouncements such as the *Imperial Rescript to Soldiers and Sailors* (1882) and the *Imperial Rescript on Education* (1890) were written to ward off foreign influence and ensure that the traditional virtues that governed the samurai were now applied to military personnel and public school students. The Meiji elites urged patriotism and social harmony to check potential dissidents, and it was to be achieved by employing the traditional myths modified to fit contemporary needs.[115]

What is critical is how the myth is portrayed. From our discussion, we have seen how the Japanese government and political elites modified and utilized Bushido. However, an individual writer can have an impact. Nitobe Inazo (1862-1933), agronomist, diplomat, politician, and writer, published his most famous book, *Bushido: The Soul of Japan*, in 1900. It was the first major work on Bushido and Japanese culture, written in English and meant for Western audiences. The book has been translated into Japanese and many other languages. It is a romanticized picture of the samurai, and to make the virtues of the samurai understandable, they are explained in terms of Western chivalry. The reaction to the book in Japan differed from that of the US. Japanese scholars criticized the work, and it was largely ignored by academia. Still, it grew in popularity, and today, Nitobe is highly regarded in Japan. His portrait was featured on the five thousand yen banknote printed from 1984 to 2004. Regarding the samurai's image, the book led to a misconception of the samurai, viewing the samurai in the traditional mold, which was far removed from the transformation that had already taken place. Despite criticism, widely disseminated and assimilated images are not easily overturned. The general public tends to hold on to the romanticized samurai myth; it persists to this day.

---

115 Gluck, *Japan's Modern*, 38-39.

It is interesting how the samurai myths have affected American writers, the media, and the public and how Americans have impacted the myths. Perhaps the writer who was the most influential on the portrayal of the samurai myths was James Clavell. Clavell spent three years researching and writing *Shogun* (1975). The book was a bestseller and was made into a six-episode, twelve-hour television miniseries in 1980. It received high ratings and had a large audience; nearly a third of American households (about 120 million viewers) watched the series. *Shogun* is a historical fiction based on the events during the Sengoku period of sixteenth-century feudal Japan. Clavell condenses the events into a single summer when they actually spanned several years. The love story of the American protagonist and a high-status Japanese woman is fictitious, as are the various subplots. Even so, the characters in the novel are drawn from historical figures. The names are changed, but it is easy to see who is being portrayed. Sex, violence, and schemes fill the novel. Clavell was criticized for overly depicting the brutality of the samurai and showing them to be barbarians. But Clavell was writing about the Sengoku era, a time of perpetual warfare, probably the most ruthless period in Japanese history. It is the actions and the political plots that capture the attention of audiences.

Akira Kurosawa loved to make movies from this period because of its battles and especially the political intrigues, which involved the universal human traits of jealousy, greed, and thirst for power. Several Kurosawa films are based on Shakespeare's handling of these human frailties. His *Throne of Blood* (1957) is inspired by *Macbeth*, and *Ran* (Chaos, 1985) is derived from *King Lear.* In the epic historical drama film *Kagemusha* (Shadow Warrior, 1980), the film ends with the spectacular Battle of Nagashino of 1575. The movie is based on the activities of the Takeda clan during the Sengoku era, and besides the battles, it relates to a series of political schemes. This turbulent time provides plenty of drama for a novelist or movie director. Clavell and Kurosawa produced excellent artistic products about this historical period, and it is understandable why their works attracted such a wide audience.

The *Shogun* television series was well-received in Japan. Japanese were impressed that, for a change, Americans did not include a lot of cliches. Nonetheless, it is a historical drama, so Clavell and the show's producers took liberties with personages and events. Historians agree there are many inaccuracies and misreadings about the ethos of the samurai, but it broadly corresponds with historical facts. For most Americans, it was their first exposure to an in-depth treatment of Japanese history and culture. Any information about the Japanese and their culture was intriguing. Clavell was fascinated with certain aspects of samurai culture, for example, eating raw fish, frequent bathing, participating in tea ceremonies, and having a natural view of sex and nudity. When the book was published, Americans began to acquire a taste for sushi (raw fish and vinegar rice), and soon after, it became a craze. Clavell believed the West could learn and perhaps adopt some practices of the Japanese culture.

In February 2024, a new version of *Shogun* aired on FX and streamed on Hulu. It was widely acclaimed, drew a massive audience, and won many Emmys. Created by Justin Marks and Rachel Kondo, the ten-episode series features a primarily Japanese cast, and most of the dialogue is in Japanese with English subtitles. Future seasons are planned due to its success. This version of *Shogun* differs from the previous series in that it focuses on the Japanese characters rather than the American protagonist. The key protagonist is Lord Toranaga Yoshii (based on Tokugawa Ieyasu, 1543-1616), played by the veteran actor Sanada Hiroyuki. Sanada was also a co-producer and advised on the authenticity of the production. Again, this is a historical drama, and the facts are embellished and exaggerated to create dramatic effects. Death by boiling is depicted. Such practices occurred in Japan but were extremely rare. The legendary bandit Ishikawa Goemon was boiled alive with his young son for his attempt to assassinate Toyotomi Hideyoshi. It is not so shocking, considering that in medieval Europe, people were executed by boiling, although this method was seldom used. There is something to be said for interest in the macabre. Today, some European towns display the kettles used in the execution of criminals. Other samurai practices such as hawking is depicted in the TV series. This is true, for hawking was a popular hobby of the warrior class.

The impact of the novel *Shogun* and its succeeding series is obvious. By focusing on a pivotal period of Japanese history, they portrayed the traditional samurai myth and the beginning stages of the transformation, bringing forth the new samurai myth. It is important to understand why and how changes occurred and the underlying realities. Clavell's *Shogun* and its successors have disseminated information about Japan and reached more people than all the combined efforts of scholars, journalists, movie directors, and other novelists.

People love stories, and they love myths. Myths affect people in different ways. Japanese have their interpretation of the cowboy myth. Many wannabe Japanese cowboys find the freedom of independence and optimistic feeling alluring. In 1993, *Samurai Cowboy*, a Canadian low-budget and low-rated film, was released. It is about a workaholic Japanese executive who gives up his hectic corporate life and moves to America to pursue his dream of becoming a cowboy. Settling down as a Montana cattle rancher, he has hopes to enjoy the wide-open countryside brimming with opportunities and experiencing the cowboy culture. As with many dreams, it does not turn out how he expected. For many Japanese, they can enjoy the cowboy culture without visiting or living in the American West. Those who seek such pleasure tend to be the older generation, who grew up watching Western movies and listening to cowboy music and are knowledgeable about the ways of the cowboy. They meet with their colleagues, all dressed in cowboy attire, to sing, dance, and have barbecue and beans from the chuck wagon. There are newspaper accounts of Japanese businessmen who gather together, wearing their cowboy outfits of hats, bandanas, Western shirts, blue jeans, leather chaps, and boots. As a group, they ride horses and practice roping. When an American observer commented that the cowboy hero, like the samurai hero, is basically a loner, the Japanese quickly corrected him. They said the cowboy worked as a group in the cattle drives and around the campfires. Cowboy means a team effort.

However, this is a misperception of the cowboy. Most cowboys suffered from wanderlust, going from one ranch to another. Only a few stayed over a year at a given ranch. They left for various reasons, and better pay was one big reason, but the large, wide-open space may have enticed them to explore the surroundings. Granted, they did work as a team while doing their job, but they had little loyalty to the ranch, their fellow workers, and the job itself. David Dary, the cowboy researcher, quotes the lyrics of a cowboy song, "The Wandering Cowboy." The beginning and ending stanzas capture the feeling of the cowboy:

I am a wandering cowboy,
From ranch to ranch I roam;
At every ranch when welcome,
I make myself at home.

...

It is now I'm tired of rambling.
No longer will I roam
When my pony I've unsaddled
In the old corral at home.[116]

The cowboy was more of a loner than a team player. However, Japan is a group-oriented society, where the group is more important than the individual. Therefore, the cowboy image had to be fitted into the Japanese way of thinking. In another arena, that of competitive sports, this difference in attitude and values can be seen. A highly paid American baseball star commented on his Japanese team doing extensive pregame and postgame practices. He said that, as a talented player, he only needs a few minutes of warmup practice before the game. The Japanese countered by saying, "You gotta have *wa*." By *wa*, Japanese means "social harmony or group harmony," working together as a team. You are loyal to the team.[117] Americans would interpret *wa* as inner harmony, be true to yourself. The perspectives of the Japanese and Americans are quite different. It did not stop the Japanese from actively seeking to take on the personage of the cowboy, even though this meant modifying the image to conform with Japanese culture.

On the other hand, Americans react differently to the samurai myth, and although intrigued by it, they do not care to take on the samurai persona. But Americans do want and seek the lifestyle of the mythical cowboy. This is clearly evident in the "Yellowstone Effect." The television series *Yellowstone,* which began in 2018, ended its run in December 2024. The highly successful program is about a cattle ranch in Montana located near Yellowstone National Park. The episodes followed the trials and challenges of a ranch family as it faced officials, neighbors, and developers. There are the familiar tropes of Western films, but it has a modern twist to fit contemporary times. Americans

116 Dary, *Cowboy,* 196-97. Quoted from John R. Craddock, "Songs the Cowboys Sing," in *Texas and Southwestern Lore* (Austin: Texas Folk-Lore Society, 1927), 190-91.

117 Robert Whiting, *You Gotta Have Wa.* 2nd ed. (New York: Vintage Departures, 2009).

are attracted to the lifestyle of the modern cowboy and the wide-open countryside. Due to the television series, there is a repeat of the pattern that took place about one hundred and fifty years ago when the cowboy myth and the vastness of the Great Plains attracted hordes of Americans to migrate. Once it began, the railroads expanded along with other facets of urbanization. Eventually, this led to the demise of the frontier and the end of the cowboys. Similarly, the large number of Americans moving into a particular area of Montana is taking away grazing land as housing developments are constructed, causing land prices to soar, and changing the economic conditions. From this experience, we see the "cowboy spirit" of the mythical cowboy to be strong and pervasive.

Thus, myths are perceived and handled differently in each country. Cowboy and samurai myths have contrasting stories on how they originated, developed, and are modified. However, in both countries, the inward aspects of the myths have continued and become an integral part of their respective cultures and even a part of their national character. In the United States and Japan, myths have endured. If you listen carefully, you might hear "yippee ki-yay" and "banzai."

GLOSSARY

anjin — "pilot;" the name for the protagonist in Clavell"s *Shogun* and the historical William Adams. Adams, a navigator, was the first Englishman in Japan and became a disseminator of information about the West. An advisor to Tokugawa Ieyasu, he was given an honorary status for his contributions.

bakafu — "tent government;" the three military governments, Kamakura, Ashikaga, and Tokugawa that ruled Japan from 1192 to1868.

bandana — probably from the Middle East or Southern Asia. It is a colorful, patterned large cloth also known as a scarf, kerchief, or wildrag. It is worn around the neck to protect from the sun and the cold and over the mouth and nose to protect from dust.

branding — a mark placed on an animal's hide by hot iron to indicate ownership. Cattle tend to wander great distances while grazing and can get lost. It was done twice a year and was a big event for the cowboys.

bronco — "rough" or "wild" in Spanish; shorten to bronc, it refers to the taming of a wild horse so it could be ridden. Bronc riding is a form of rodeo competition.

bu — military arts; the duty of the samurai was to cultivate his martial skills as stated in clan instructions and other writings.

buckaroo — corruption of the Spanish word *vaquero*. It is synonymous with cowboy, but some make the distinction between the buckaroo of California and the cowboy of Texas.

bun —literary arts; in tandem with *bu,* samurai were encouraged to participate in literary activities, and in other cultural activities such as painting and tea ceremony.

bunraku —puppet play; began in the Edo period and uses puppeteers, chanters, and musicians. Many of the themes comes from *kabuki* such as the story of the forty-seven *ronin.*

bushidan — local band of warriors from related families. A kinship-based organization, it was the forerunner of the samurai.

Bushido — "the Way of the Warrior;" ethical code of the samurai class formalized during the Edo period. It includes virtues of loyalty, honor, duty, and courage.

chambara — sword fighting in Japanese cinema.

chaps — leather leggings of Mexican Spanish origin. Worn over the trousers to protect against thorns and needles of plants while riding.

chuck wagon — wagon carrying equipment and provisions for cooking on the cattle drive. Today, it is used to describe outdoor buffet dining.

chushin gishi — "loyal and dutiful samurai;" concept of giving one's life for a greater cause as in a retainer sacrificing his life out of duty and loyalty to his lord.

Chushingura — "The Treasury of Loyal Retainers;" originally a fourteenth century story, the characters and events were similar to the forty-seven *ronin* incident. Playwrights made the changes. and it became a fictionalized account of the real vendetta. It started as a *bunraku* and then became famous as a *kabuki* play. It has been made into several novels, films, and television series.

daimyo — feudal lord with a domain yielding a minimal income of ten thousand *koku.*

daiso — "large and small;" matched pair of swords worn by the samurai.

Dejima — man-made island off Nagasaki that served as a trading post for the Portuguese and later the Dutch. For over two hundred years, it was the only opening for Westerners.

drover — synonymous with driver; cowboy who drives cattle.

gekokujo — "the lower overthrows the higher;" where the retainers overthrew their lord. During the Sengoku period, retainers rebelled against the immoral behavior of their lord. In modern times, applied to military factions going against orders and taking independent actions.

gyokusai — "shattered jewels;" the word comes from an ancient Chinese text. It refers to group suicide or suicidal mission as in "banzai charge" and kamikaze attack.

harakiri — common term for ritual suicide by disembowelment. See *seppuku*.

hatamono — bannerman; high-ranking samurai directly under the Tokugawa shogun, they had the right to an audience with the shogun.

Hirado — island off the northwest coast of Kyushu near Nagasaki. It was a port for trade with the West in the sixteenth and seventeenth centuries. The Dutch were the principal occupier but were forced to move to Dejima in 1641.

jidaigeki — "period dramas;" a genre of Japanese films, television series, and plays based on fictionalized stories in historical settings.

jizamurai — "samurai of the land;" were lower-ranking samurai who were farmers but when called upon, served as foot soldiers. Eventually, they were given the choice of moving into castle towns or forsaking their samurai status and becoming peasant farmers.

junshi — "following the lord in death;" the practice of retainers committing suicide upon the death of their lord. It was practiced so widely, many *daimyo* banned it and eventually the Tokugawa shogunate outlawed it.

kabuto —type of helmet first used by ancient warriors but later became part of traditional samurai armor. Higher rank samurai had decorative crest and symbol in the front of their helmet in the shape of sun, moon, flames, and even antler.

kaishakunin — "decapitation assistant;" the person who stands behind and makes the finishing cut at the neck during the *seppuku* to end the pain of the suffering samurai.

kaku — house or clan ethical instructions for the samurai.

katana — long sword worn by the samurai. Ideal for close combat because of its sharpness, strength, and longer reach.

kawaraban — single-sheet woodblock print.

koku —measurement unit, where one koku equals five US bushels. The income derived from the land is measured by its productivity in koku of rice. One koku of rice purportedly supports one person for a year. See *kokudaka*.

kokudaka — productivity assessment. A measure of wealth of a domain based on the annual yield in units of *koku* of rice. It was an easier and simpler way of determining wealth than by using money. See *koku*.

Kokugaku — "national study;" philosophic school and scholarly movement of the Tokugawa period, and by focusing on Japanese scholarship, it is a departure from Chinese studies.

kokutai — "national polity;" nebulous term appearing in late Tokugawa period, it refers to the "national identity or character" of Japan. It has been used by Japanese nationalists to point out Japan's uniqueness and hence its superiority to other countries.

kubi jikken — "head-viewing ceremony;" where the lord would inspect the severed heads of the defeated enemy. A record was kept and could be the bases for promotion and rewards.

lariat — long light rope with a running noose. It is utilized to catch cattle. The word is used as a noun.

lasso — rope without noose. The word is usually used as a verb.

makoto — "sincerity;" it is one of the virtues in the Bushido. Motive is important and determines whether the action is correct.

maverick — derived from the name of a rancher who did not brand his cattle and thereby caused confusion. The word refers to an individual who does not go along with the group.

mustang — wild horses of the western plains descended from horses brought in by the Spaniards. Once they were "broken in," they were used by Native Americans and cowboys.

naginata — "mowing down sword;" a pole weapon with a long curved blade on the end. It was used by foot soldiers and were effective in dismounting and disabling the samurai.

Neo-Confucianism — a rational, social, and ethical Chinese philosophy, it was a secular form of Confucianism. The height of its influence was during the Tokugawa period, especially on hierarchical relationships and on filial piety.

ninja — "one who is invisible;" the historical ninja were mainly experts in intelligence, but their role has been idealized to experts in espionage, sabotage and assassination. *Daimyo* employed *ninja* extensively but they were considered outlier by the samurai.

ninjutsu — "the art of stealth;" techniques practiced by the *ninja*. It is used in scouting and intelligence gathering. Direct confrontation is voided by employing the stealth techniques of disguise and deception.

paniola — derived from the Spanish word *espaniola*. These Hawaiian cowboys were formed with the help of Mexican *vaqueros* and are on the Big Island of Hawai'i.

rangaku — "Dutch learning;" the principal source of knowledge about Western science and technology when Japan was isolated from the world for about two hundred years.

rodeo — from the Spanish word *rodear,* meaning "to surround or roundup." Vaqueros rounded up wild cattle and in the process developed skills in roping, bull riding and wrestling, and broc riding. These skills were demonstrated and became competitive contests in a show called rodeo.

ronin — masterless samurai. A samurai became a ronin upon the death of his lord or the lord's lost of his domain.

roundup — the operation each spring and fall to gather the cattle that had strayed into the open range, and then to sort the cattle and return them to their owners. The new calves were branded and those destined for the market were driven away.

ryu — mainly used as a suffix, but by itself means a school of martial arts. It is the tradition and not the building.

sakoku — the isolationist foreign policy of the Tokugawa government, severely restricting relations with other countries and banning Japanese from leaving the country.

sankin-kotai — "alternate attendance;" a policy of the Tokugawa shogunate requiring *daimyo* to reside every other year in Edo, the capital of the shogunate. It was designed to control and weaken the *daimyo.* The dual residences and the journeys to and from Edo drained the domain's finances.

seppuku — "cutting the belly;" the formal term for what is commonly known in the the West as *harakiri.* This ritual suicide by disembowelment was originally reserved for the samurai but in modern times others have practiced it. Usually performed with an assistant who decapitates the samurai at the same moment to end the pain. See *kaishakunin.*

shinai — a sword made of bamboo used for martial arts practice and competition. Light and flexible, it is designed to prevent serious injury.

shinobi — "one who sneaks;" it is synonymous with *ninja*. *Ninja* is a term familiar to American readers, whereas *shinobi* is unfamiliar and not often used in Western writings. See ninja.

shogunate — it is synonymous and is the English version of *bakafu*. It is the government of the *shogun*, the military ruler of Japan. See *bakafu*.

taiga drama — televised year-long series of historical drama.

tanegashima — when not capitalized, it is the matchlock rifle, the first firearm discovered by the Japanese; named after the island where it was found.

Texas fever — a disease caused by cattle ticks carried by the longhorns. The longhorns were immune to the disease, but the livestock of the regions along the trail drive were affected.

vaquero — "cow worker" in Spanish. They are Mexican cowboys from whose tradition the American cowboys emanates.

wakizashi — "side inserted sword;" is the shorter of two swords worn by the samurai. It is considered a sidearm and is used in *seppuku*. It is better suited for indoor fighting because it requires shorter motions.

yabusame — is a type of mounted archery. When the samurai became prominent, they fought on horseback with the bow, which was the principal weapon. Shooting the bow while galloping on horseback requires considerable skill. Today, this practice has become a ritual and is performed for special ceremonies or events.

yari — long spear with an extended narrow double edged blade. It became important in the fifteenth century when armies were larger with more foot soldiers and fought in tighter formation. It replaced the *naginata* and in turn was downgraded by firearms in the Edo period.

yoke — a shaped pattern piece attached at the top of shirt or at the shoulder. It gives a broad shoulder appearance and is now associated with the cowboy image.

yumi — long bow; it was the main weapon of the mounted samurai for a long period until undermined by the *yari* and *tanegashima*. It still maintains its importance in *yabusame* and in the sport of archery (*kyudo*).

Zen Buddhism — it appealed to the samurai because it did not have the elaborate rituals and scriptures of the other Buddhist sects and instead focused on mental discipline and simplicity of practice. It influenced Bushido, and its meditative aspect created interest in painting, tea ceremony, calligraphy, rock garden, and martial arts.

BIBLIOGRAPHY

Adams, Ramon F. and Homer E. Britzman. *Charles M. Russell: The Cowboy Artist - A Biography.* Pasadena, CA: Trail's End Publishing,1948.

Agnew, Jeremy. *The Creation of the Cowboy Hero: Fiction, Film and Fact.* Jefferson, NC: McFarland, 2015.

Agnew, Jeremy. *The Old West in Fact and Film: History Versus Hollywood.* Jefferson, NC: McFarland, 2012.

Assmann, Cody. *History of the West with Sam Payne: Trail to Cheyenne.* Self-published, 2022.

Bargen, Doris G. *Suicidal Honor: General Nogi and the Writings of Mori Ogai and Natsume Soseki.* Honolulu: University of Hawai'i Press, 2006.

Beasley, W.G. *The Japanese Experience: A Short History of Japan.* Berkeley: University of California Press, 1999.

Benesch, Oleg. *Inventing the Way of the Samurai: Nationalism, Internationalism and Bushido in Modern Japan.* New York: Oxford University Press, 2014.

Buchanan, Daniel Crump, ed., *Japanese Proverbs and Sayings.* Norman, OK: University of Oklahoma Press, 1965.

Campbell, Joseph. *The Hero with a Thousand Faces*. 3rd ed. Novato, CA: New World Library, 2008.

Carlson, Paul H., ed. *The Cowboy Way: An Exploration of History and Culture*. Lubbock, TX: Texas Tech University Press, 2006.

Carlson, Paul H. "Myth and the Modern Cowboy." In chap. 1 of *The Cowboy Way: An Exploration of History and Culture*, ed. Paul H. Carlson. Lubbock, TX: Texas Tech University Press, 2006.

Chrisman, Harry E. *Lost Trails of the Cimarron*. 2nd ed. Norman, OK: University of Oklahoma Press, 1964.

Clayton, Lawrence, Jim Hoy, and Jerald Underwood. *Vaqueros, Cowboys, and Buckaroos*. Austin, TX: University of Texas Press, 2001.

Cummins, Antony and Yoshie Minami, trans. *The Book of Ninja: The First Complete Translation of the Bansenshukai*. London: Watkins, 2013.

Dary, David. *Cowboy Culture: A Saga of Five Centuries*. Lawrence, KS: University Press of Kansas, 1989.

de Bary, Wm. Theodore, ed. *Sources of Japanese Tradition*. New York: Columbia University Press, 1958.

Dobie, J. Frank. *The Longhorns*. Illustrated by Tom Lea. Austin, TX: University of Texas Press, 2000.

Donway, Walter. "Fukuzawa Yukichi: The Man Who Was 'Civilization and Enlightenment' in Japan." The Reading Room. December 8, 2022. oll.libertyfund.org > reading-room > 202…

Doug, John. *In Search of Japan's Hidden Christians: A Story of Suppression, Secrecy and Survival*. Rutland, VT: Tuttle Publishing, 2012.

Dower, John W. "Black Ships & Samurai: Commodore Perry and the Opening of Japan (1853-1854)." Cambridge, MA: Visualizing Cultures, Massachusetts Institute of Technology, 2010. visualizingcultures.mit.educ > black_ships…

Dower, John W. *Ways of Forgetting, Ways of Remembering: Japan in the Modern World*. New York: New Press, 2012.

Dykstra, Robert R. *The Cattle Towns.* Lincoln, NE: University of Nebraska Press, 1983.

Earl, David M. "Yamaga Soko" In vol. 8, *290. Kodansha Encyclopedia of Japan.* Tokyo: Kodansha, 1983.

Endo, Shusaku. *Silence.* Translated by William Johnston. New York: Picador Modern Classics, 1969.

Feiler, Bruce S. *Learning to Bow: Inside the Heart of Japan.* New York: Perennial, 2004.

Frantz, Joe B. and Julian Ernest Choate, Jr. *The American Cowboy: The Myth and the Reality.* Norman, OK: University of Oklahoma Press, 1955.

Fujitani, Takashi. *Splendid Monarchy and Pageantry in Modern Japan.* Berkeley: University of California Press, 1998.

Glasrud, Bruce A. and Michael N. Searles, eds. *Black Cowboys in the American West: On the Range, on the Stage, behind the Badge.* Norman, OK: University of Oklahoma Press, 2016.

Gluck, Carol. *Japan's Modern Myths: Ideology in the Late Meiji Period.* Princeton, NJ: Princeton University Press, 1985.

Grayling, Christopher. *Spaghetti Westerns: Cowboys and Europeans from Karl May to Sergio Leone.* 2nd ed. New York: I.B. Tauris, 2006.

Hales, Douglas. "Black Cowboy: Daniel Webster '80 John' Wallace." In Glasrud, *Black Cowboys,* 75-84. Also in Carlson, *The Cowboy Way,* 33-43.

Harris, Charles W. and Buck Rainey, eds. *The Cowboy: Six-Shooters, Songs, and Sex.* Norman, OK: University of Oklahoma Press, 1976.

Hobsbawm, Eric. "The Myth of the Cowboy." *The Guardian.* March 20, 2013. www.theguardian.com > profile > eric_ho…

Hobsbawm, Eric and Terence Ranger, eds. *The Invention of Tradition.* Cambridge, UK: Cambridge University Press, 1983.

Hunter, John Marvin, ed. *The Trail Drivers of Texas.* New York: Argosy-Antiquarian Press, 1963.

Isenberg, Andrew C. *Wyatt Earp: A Vigilante Life*. New York: Hill and Wang, 2013.

Jansen, Marius B. *Sakamoto Ryoma and the Meiji Restoration*. New York: Columbia University Press, 1994.

Kakehashi, Kumiko. *So Sad to Fall in Battle: An Account of War*. New York: Presidio Press, 2007.

Karp, Aaron. "Estimating Global Civilian-held Firearms Numbers." Small Arms Survey Briefing Paper, June 2018. www.smallarmssurvey.org > files.

Knowles, Elizabeth, ed. *The Oxford Dictionary of Quotations*. 5th ed. New York: Oxford University Press, 1999. vol. 8. Tokyo: Kodansha, 1983.

Kohn, Abigail A. *Shooters: Myths and Realities of America's Gun Cultures*. New York: Oxford University Press, 2004.

Kuribayashi, Tadamichi. *"Gyokusai soshikikan" no etegami*. Tokyo: Shogakkan, 2002.

Lederer, William J. and Eugene Burdick. *The Ugly American*. New York: W.W. Norton & Company, 1958.

Lee, Gregory M., ed., *Ideals of the Samurai: Writings of Japanese Warriors*. Translated and introduction by William Scott Wilson. Santa Clarita, CA: Ohara Publications, 1982.

Lifton, Robert Jay, Shuichi Kato and Micheal R. Reich. *Six Lives, Six Deaths: Portraits from Modern Japan*. New Haven: Yale University Press, 1979.

Lipset, Seymour Martin. "Pacific Divide: American Exceptionalism—Japanese Uniqueness." *International Journal of Public Opinion Research,* vol. 5, no. 2, Summer 1993, 121-166.

Lomax, John Avery, ed. *Cowboy Songs and Other Frontier Ballads*. New York: Macmillan, 1922.

Lustbader, Eric Van. *The Ninja*. London: Grafton Books, 1980.

Marty, Myron. "Lincoln Legends: Myths, Hoaxes, and Confabulations Associated with Our Greatest President by Edward Steers Jr."

Journal of the Abraham Lincoln Association 30, issue 1 (Winter 2009): 74-79.

Morris, Ivan N. *The Nobility of Failure: Tragic Heroes in the History of Japan.* New York: Holt, Rinehart and Winston, 1945.

McCullough, Helen Craig, *The Taiheiki: A Chronicle of Medieval Japan.* Rutland, VT: Tuttle Publishing, 1979.

McMurtry, Larry. *Lonesome Dove: A Novel.* New York: Simon & Schuster, 1985.

Minichiello, Sharon A., ed. *Japan's Competing Modernities: Issues in Culture and Democracy, 1900-1930.* Honolulu: University of Hawai'i Press, 1998.

Mishima, Yukio. *On Hagakure: The Samurai Ethic and Modern Japan.* Translated by Kathryn Starling. Tokyo: Charles E. Tuttle, 1978.

Neff, Emily Ballew. *The Modern West: American Landscapes, 1890-1950.* New Haven:Yale University Press, 2006.

Okuma, Shigenobu. *Fifty Years of New Japan.* 1st ed., vol. II. London: Smith, Elder, 1909-10.

Ravina, Mark. *The Last Samurai: The Life and Battles of Saigo Takamori.* Hoboken, NJ: John Wiley & Sons, Inc., 2004.

Reynolds, Bill. "Cowboy Codes from Western Heroes." *Western Horseman*, October 4, 2017. western<u>horseman.com</u> > culture > out-west.

Ridings, Sam P. *The Chisholm Trail: A History of the World's Greatest Cattle Trail.* New York: Skyhorse Publishing, 2015.

Rosa, Joseph G. *Wild Bill Hickok, Gunfighter: An Account of Hickok's Gunfights.* Norman. OK: University of Oklahoma Press, 2003.

Rosa, Joseph G. and Robin May. *Buffalo Bill and His Wild West: A Pictorial Biography.* Lawrence, KS: University Press of Kansas, 1989.

Sansom, George Bailey. *A History of Japan to 1334.* Stanford: Stanford University Press, 1958.

Sato, Hiroaki. "Gyokusai or 'Shattering Like a Jewel:' Reflection on the Pacific War. *Asia-Pacific Journal.* Japan Focus. February 1, 2008. apjjf.org > hiroaki-sato > article.

Sato, Hiroaki. *Legends of the Samurai.* New York: Overlook Duckworth, 1995.

Satow, Ernest Mason. *A Diplomat in Japan.* London: Seeley, Service, 1921.

Savage, William W., Jr. *The Cowboy Hero: His Image in American History and Culture.* Norman, OK: University of Oklahoma Press, 1979.

Segal, Robert A., ed. *Jung on Mythology.* Princeton, NJ: Princeton University Press, 1998.

Segal, Robert A. *Theorizing About Myth.* Amherst, MA: University of Massachusetts Press, 1999.

Sell, Henry Blackman and Victor Weybright. *Buffalo Bill and the Wild West.* New York: Oxford University Press, 1955.

Smith, Henry, ed., *Learning from Shogun: Japanese History and Western Fantasy.* Santa Barbara, CA: Program in Asian Studies, University of California, Santa Barbara, 1980.

Starrs, Roy. "Writing the National Narrative: Changing Attitudes toward Nation-Building among Japanese Writers, 1900-1930." In Minichiello, *Japan's Competing Modernities,* 206-27.

Steers, Edward Jr. *Lincoln Legends: Myths, Hoaxes, and Confabulations Associated with Our Greatest President.* Lexington, KY: The University Press of Kentucky, 2007.

Takii, Kazuhiro. *Ito Hirobumi - Japan's First Prime Minister and Father of the Meiji Constitution.* Translated by Takechi Manabu. New York: Routledge, 2014.

Taliaferro, John. *Charles M. Russell: The Life and Legend of America's Cowboy Artist.* Norman, OK: University of Oklahoma Press, 2003.

Turnbull, Stephen. *The Lone Samurai and the Martial Arts.* London: Arms and Armour, 1992.

Underwood, Jerald. "The Vaquero." In Clayton, *Vaqueros,* 1-66.

Whiting, Robert. *You Gotta Have Wa.* 2nd ed. New York: Vintage Departures, 2009.

Wister, Owen. *The Virginian: A Horseman of the Plains.* New York: Macmillan, 1902.

Wright, Will. *Six Guns and Society: A Structural Study of the Western.* Berkeley, University of California Press, 1975.

Yamamoto, Tsunetomo. *The Pocket Hagakure: The Book of the Samurai.* Translated by William Scott Wilson. Boulder, CO: Shambhala Publications, 2019.

ABOUT THE AUTHOR

Minoru Yanagihashi has a lifelong interest in Japanese and American history and culture. He holds degrees from the University of Hawai'i (BA), University of Washington (MLS), University of California, Berkeley (MA), and University of Michigan (PhD). Before his academic career, he served as an infantry officer in South Korea and was a reference librarian at California State University in Los Angeles. He has taught at several universities, including the University of Michigan and the University of Arizona. Although his specialty is Japanese politics and foreign relations, he has written about the experiences of Japanese Americans and has been involved with and documented cultural development.

www.ingramcontent.com/pod-product-compliance
Lightning Source LLC
Chambersburg PA
CBHW021623120626
46545CB00001B/373